PEB

PROGRAMME ON EDUCATIONAL BUILDING

DECENTRALISATION AND EDUCATIONAL BUILDING MANAGEMENT:

The Impact of Recent Reforms

ORGANISATION FOR ECONOMIC CO-OPERATION AND DEVELOPMENT

ORGANISATION FOR ECONOMIC CO-OPERATION AND DEVELOPMENT

Pursuant to Article 1 of the Convention signed in Paris on 14th December 1960, and which came into force on 30th September 1961, the Organisation for Economic Co-operation and Development (OECD) shall promote policies designed:

- to achieve the highest sustainable economic growth and employment and a rising standard of living in Member countries, while maintaining financial stability, and thus to contribute to the development of the world economy;
- to contribute to sound economic expansion in Member as well as non-member countries in the process of economic development; and
- to contribute to the expansion of world trade on a multilateral, non-discriminatory basis in accordance with international obligations.

The original Member countries of the OECD are Austria, Belgium, Canada, Denmark, France, Germany, Greece, Iceland, Ireland, Italy, Luxembourg, the Netherlands, Norway, Portugal, Spain, Sweden, Switzerland, Turkey, the United Kingdom and the United States. The following countries became Members subsequently through accession at the dates indicated hereafter: Japan (28th April 1964), Finland (28th January 1969), Australia (7th June 1971) and New Zealand (29th May 1973). The Commission of the European Communities takes part in the work of the OECD (Article 13 of the OECD Convention).

The Programme on Educational Building (PEB) was established by the Council of the Organisation for Economic Co-operation and Development as from January 1972. Its present mandate expires at the end of 1996.

The main objectives of the Programme are:

- to facilitate the exchange of information and experience on aspects of educational building judged to be important by participating Member countries;
- to promote co-operation between such Member countries regarding the technical bases for improving the quality, speed and cost effectiveness of school construction.

The Programme functions within the Directorate for Education, Employment, Labour and Social Affairs of the Organisation in accordance with the decisions of the Council of the Organisation, under the authority of the Secretary-General. It is directed by a Steering Committee of senior government officials, and financed by participating governments.

Publié en français sous le titre :
LA DÉCENTRALISATION
ET LES LOCAUX SCOLAIRES

© OECD 1992
Applications for permission to reproduce or translate all or part of this publication should be made to:
Head of Publications Service, OECD
2, rue André-Pascal, 75775 PARIS CEDEX 16, France

Table of Contents

Foreword 5
Preface 7

Part One

THE PLANNING AND FUNDING OF EDUCATIONAL BUILDING

Introduction... 11
Recent Experience in Five Countries 13
Conference Conclusions 37
Note on Central and Eastern Europe 43

Part Two

CONFERENCE PAPERS

Welcoming Address 47
Resource Allocation and Educational Quality 51
Resourcing the Curriculum: Furniture and Equipment 57
Resource Allocation for New Construction and Maintenance 63
Building for Quality: An Architect's View 67
Building for Quality: A Builder's View 71
Maintenance Planning... 73
Energy Management.. 77

Annex: Issues for Discussion at the Conference.............. 81

Notes on Authors... 84

ALSO AVAILABLE

PEB Exchange. *Newsletter of the Programme on Educational Building*
(88 00 00 1)
Subscription No 15 to No 17 FF125 £14.00 US$30.00 DM48
Schools and Quality. An International Report (1989)
(91 89 02 1) ISBN 92-64-13254-6 FF95 £11.50 US$20.00 DM39

Prices charged at the OECD Bookshop.
THE OECD CATALOGUE OF PUBLICATIONS and supplements will be sent free of charge on request addressed either to OECD Publications Service, or to the OECD Distributor in your country.

Foreword

Decentralisation from national to local government, and from government at all levels to individuals and institutions, has had a significant impact on education systems, and in particular on the construction and management of schools. This report is the outcome of an international conference on "Trends in the Planning and Funding of Educational Building" which was jointly organised by the OECD Programme on Educational Building and the Ministry of Education and Science of the Netherlands in October 1990. The main purpose of the conference was to enable participants, through the exchange of ideas and information, to analyse the effects on educational building of recent reforms in the administration of education. The report looks at the legislative and administrative framework within which schools are planned and built, at the way in which resources are allocated for their construction and maintenance, and at how they are run on a day-to-day basis.

The author of the synthesis report and conclusions is Thierry Malan, Inspecteur général de l'Administration in the French Ministry of Education. The opinions he expresses are his own and do not necessarily reflect the views of the OECD. This volume is published on the responsibility of the Secretary-General of the OECD.

Preface

In response to current developments in a number of countries the OECD Programme on Educational Building (PEB) and the Netherlands Ministry of Education and Science jointly organised an international conference on "Trends in the Planning and Funding of Educational Building".

The conference, which took place in October 1990 at Noordwijkerhout in the Netherlands, provided the opportunity for an exchange of knowledge and views on the ins and outs of systems for planning and funding educational building in OECD countries.

PEB commissioned case-studies in five Member countries: France, the Netherlands, Norway, Portugal and the United Kingdom. The results of these studies, together with experts' accounts of Dutch attitudes towards resource allocation systems and the demands they have to meet, were presented as a basis for discussion. An analysis of these contributions and the final conclusions of the conference are published in this report.

Special attention was paid to the participation of observers from Central and Eastern Europe at the conference. As the delegates from the Czech and Slovak Federal Republic, Hungary and Poland confirmed, it was for them a unique opportunity to acquire the knowledge needed to initiate new forms of cooperation between authorities and schools in their countries, which are in the process of building pluralist constitutional states and market economies.

We hope that this report will prove useful for those involved in planning and managing educational buildings at all levels, and that it will help give shape to new and more adequate systems which will contribute to the attainment of ever higher educational standards.

The Minister of Education and Science

Dr. Jo M. M. Ritzen

Part One

THE PLANNING AND FUNDING OF EDUCATIONAL BUILDING

Introduction

Most OECD countries have recently made important changes in the distribution of responsibilities for the planning, funding, and management of educational buildings. In many cases these have taken the form of a decentralisation of important areas of decision-making to local authorities. The OECD Programme on Educational Building undertook a study of some of the implications of these developments for the education service. The findings of the study were discussed at a conference in the Netherlands in 1990.

Part One of this report provides a synthesis of recent developments in the five countries studied, together with the conference conclusions. Although each of the educational systems studied is unique, the issues that they face are common to very many countries. Part Two of the report consists of a number of papers presented at the conference. They deal in more detail with aspects of educational building management, drawing particularly on Dutch experience. They are included not only for their intrinsic interest, but in order to show how the day-to-day running and management of educational (and indeed other) buildings is irrevocably linked to the initial capital investment, and that it is essential to provide adequately for maintenance if the very substantial investments that have been made, and are being made, in educational buildings in all countries, are not to be allowed to deteriorate. The following extracts from the introductory talk given by Mr George Papadopoulos, then Deputy Director for Education at the OECD, serve to set the study in its broader context.

"In the last five years OECD's educational activities have focused on two central concerns. One is the need, which all Member countries face, to adjust to the requirements of structural change in their economies. Structural change arises from economic necessity, in a world where national economies are increasingly interdependent, and where it is necessary to increase competitiveness. This implies, amongst other things, the development of skills and competences to facilitate competitivity, and the recognition that human beings are the most valuable resource that the industrialised countries possess. The development of human resources means improvements in the education and training systems through which human skills and competences are developed.

"The second, and related, concern is with the quality of education. When one speaks of quality one inevitably raises questions of effectiveness, and beyond that, of efficiency. The idea of efficiency introduces an economic dimension into the notion of effectiveness, which is often interpreted in purely pedagogical terms. In today's economic conditions, when financial constraints weigh heavily on governments at all levels, efficiency is frequently invoked. Education systems at all levels are called to be more accountable for the resources they use. There is a need for monitoring and evaluation and a new emphasis on the management of educational resources.

"The effective management of resources is important at all levels of the system, from the individual school, through the different layers of administration, to central ministries of education. No consideration of effective resource management can take place unless we take into account how decision-making processes at various levels operate. When we do that we come directly to the issue of decentralisation.

"Decentralisation affects not only educational building but all aspects of education: teachers, the curriculum, funding, the formal sector of education and beyond, in business, industry and the community. This should not surprise us, because we have learned, in our political philosophy as well as our business practice, that the best way to improve the effectiveness of services is to look at them at the point of delivery. That is where effectiveness is judged, in education as in other spheres.

"There is therefore a philosophy behind decentralisation. Going to the point of delivery however means more than granting people the right to manage the resources allocated to them. If it is going to be effective it should include giving them a role in defining their own needs. In increasingly pluralistic societies, where there are many different interests, the definition of the needs of individual communities is not at all easy. There may also be a hidden agenda to decentralisation. In the face of the impossibility of resolving the massive and increasing demands which are made on resources, the temptation for central government is to offload the problem on to individual localities, so that they take some of the blame when expectations are not met.

"There is also a reaction to decentralisation. If individual localities have greater responsibility then there will be a greater need for cohesion and conformity to national norms and standards. This in turn leads to more monitoring, evaluation and accounting, mostly based on quantitative techniques. The situation becomes polarised: on the one hand there is decentralisation of decision-making responsibility, on the other there is the need to meet national standards, which tend to reinforce central powers.

"Finally there is the question of equity. A poorer region which is short of resources is often unable to devote as much money to school building as its neighbours. It then becomes incumbent on central government, if its policy is to ensure the delivery of the same quality of service across the country as a whole, to apply some form of positive discrimination in the distribution of national resources to ensure that its policy is applied. Decentralisation does not mean disinterest.

"Governments can help to ensure quality, efficiency and equity in decentralised systems. Municipalities and institutions which are now able to make their own decisions are often very short of reliable information and advice on which to base them. There is a need for organisations which can promote research and development, and act as a focus for collective knowledge and wisdom, not only nationally but internationally. Central government can meet this need, not in order to impose its own will but to provide support and to channel information, which will facilitate development and progress.

"Let us not forget that what we are concerned with in education is the quality of the process itself, over and above its outcomes. The environment within which the educational process takes place, the physical entity known as the school, is of very considerable importance."

Recent Experience in Five Countries

A Synthesis Report by Thierry Malan

In recent years many countries have seen major changes both in the planning and funding of building, and in the management of educational institutions. It was felt worthwhile to form a general picture of recent and planned developments in a limited but representative sample of countries. In view of their different experiences, England, France, Norway, the Netherlands, and Portugal were selected as subjects for the study. A case-study was made of each country; the authors worked independently, but using a common set of questions. This chapter is a synthesis of their reports. Information on recent reforms in the former Federal Republic of Germany, Greece and New Zealand has also been incorporated.

The implications of these changes in the field of educational building are addressed at various levels of responsibility (national, regional, local, and institutional) and with reference to different aspects of the system - planning procedures, methods of resource allocation, administrative structures and decision-making processes, methods of management and the role of units responsible for research, dissemination of information and experimentation.

General aims of educational planning

The main legislative and regulatory measures, and the objectives of educational policies and development plans, have direct and indirect effects on the scale of the needs for educational building and the types of building required.

In recent years quantitative objectives (trends in participation rates and pupil numbers, teacher-pupil ratios) and qualitative objectives (new course options, timetables, curricula, educational structures and methods) have given rise to new requirement patterns.

Social demand and enrolment rates

A growing proportion of pupils continue their studies beyond compulsory education. Social demand, more stringent requirements in respect of qualifications on the labour market and the rate of unemployment among young people are all factors tending to prolong the duration of education.

- In Norway, for example, 95 per cent of pupils expect to continue their studies after completion of compulsory schooling.
- In France an ambitious target for increasing school enrolment has been announced: the aim is to increase to 80 per cent the proportion of pupils continuing to the end of secondary schooling. This target has substantial support across the various political parties.

A similar growth in demand is also apparent among adults already in working life, with the large-scale development of continuing education – both vocational, to meet the needs of business and industry – and more general. Much of this demand will be met by schools, generating a need for more space and for buildings to be adapted to requirements.

Structural reforms in education

Reforms in educational systems have direct and indirect implications for educational building. First amongst these is the extension of schooling and changes in the educational profile of schools.

- In France the raising of the school-leaving age to 16 and the gradual introduction of the *collège unique* (first four-year cycle of secondary education) have brought about the large-scale construction of a new type of establishment. Industrial building methods have been extensively used to speed up the rate of construction and to bring down costs. Demographic changes have made it possible to reduce the size of classes. The main pressure in terms of student intake now centres on the *lycées* (second cycle of secondary education) and on higher education. *Collège* classrooms are often used for *lycée* classes.
- In England, educational building has been influenced, among other things, by the comprehensive school movement in the 1960s and 1970s, and by the promotion of technical and vocational education in the 1980s.
- In Norway the accent has been on vocational education: of the 35 000 upper secondary school places built between 1982 and 1985, with the help of central government grants to the counties, three-quarters were for vocational training.

The development of alternate training and work experience, by altering the respective involvement and roles of the education system and business and industry as places of education, may also cause changes in requirements for premises.

Curricular change

Where national curricula drawn up by the Ministry of Education have existed for a long time (France), or have recently been introduced (Norway), requirements can be deduced from forecasts of pupil numbers and the educational structures (timetables, norms for pupil group sizes) needed for the implementation of such curricula.

- The possibility of local adjustments (of the order of 10-15 per cent of timetables and curricula) and additional courses introduced by the local authorities (France) may also involve the provision of premises.
- After a long period during which local authorities and schools in England enjoyed a considerable degree of autonomy in respect of curricula and teaching methods,

moderated to some extent by the defining of examination content at national level, the 1988 Education Reform Act introduced a system of national curricula. In many local authorities and schools this will bring about changes in the relative importance of the various subjects taught, as room is made for compulsory subjects, and will create a need for new accommodation allied to the modernisation of existing buildings.

Existing educational establishments have to be reorganised at regular intervals in order to adjust to educational developments and allow the updating of equipment. The design of new schools has to keep pace with this development and not lag behind. In France workshops will need to be installed in *collèges* in conjunction with the introduction of technology courses. The modernisation of the vocational *lycées* and the creation of new diplomas such as the *baccalauréat professionel,* are generating new equipment needs.

Pedagogical methods and safety standards

Changes in pedagogical methods, or in health and safety legislation can create new problems for the organisation of the educational environment:
- Teachers in different countries do not have the same obligations of attendance in their establishment or the same definition of their service obligations. Where they do not have to attend on a full-time basis, changes in their working conditions, incentives to work more as a team, to spend more time in school and to be more available to the pupils, presuppose the existence of facilities for individual work and meetings (France, Norway).
- Diversification in educational methods, working alone or in groups of different sizes by combining or splitting classes, creates the need for variety and flexibility in classroom types.
- Diversification in the pattern of school life is creating a new demand for documentation centres, clubs, meeting rooms, and leisure centres for pupils.
- Special arrangements have to be made in some areas for cleaning, air conditioning, cable ducting, prevention of accidents, and the prevention of theft and damage, to permit the proper use of new and costly equipment (computers, audiovisual equipment, workshop facilities).
- New regulations regarding the adaptation of premises are being introduced to facilitate the integration of disabled children into the mainstream educational process.

Institutional autonomy

This period has also seen the emergence of a desire for the redistribution of roles between local or regional authorities and their educational establishments. This has resulted in changes in the division of power, usually, but not always, in the direction of more decentralisation and greater autonomy for the schools.

Major changes of this kind in decision-making structures and the division of responsibilities between central and local authorities are also reflected in the planning and administration of education and educational building both at the central government level itself and between the central and decentralised levels. Growth in demand, increasing costs and concern for administrative efficiency have prompted the authorities to seek partners and cooperative arrangements with other actors on the educational scene.

- In England, the government has since 1975 involved local authorities in the debate on priorities for educational planning by means of a consultative committee consisting of representatives of the local authorities. In 1988, by contrast, the powers of central government in relation to those of the local authorities were enhanced by the adoption of a national curriculum, the development of the City Technology Colleges (CTC) and the possibility of establishing grant-maintained schools over which the local authorities no longer have control.
- The opposite direction was taken in France with the 1982 and 1983 Education Acts, which transferred to the *régions* and *départements,* respectively, responsibility for the building and physical operation of *lycées* and *collèges.* In order to cope with the increase in demand, the regions are now even being asked to invest more in the field of post-secondary education, which is primarily the responsibility of central government.
- In Norway, central control began in 1976 to give way to increased power for local authorities. A system of block grants was introduced, but the effective transfer of powers was phased in over a long period.
- The Netherlands also plans to transfer responsibility for the administration of state schools to the local authorities.

At the same time, developments are taking place with respect to the autonomy of educational establishments. There is a long tradition of school independence in England and the Netherlands. In other countries it is a more recent experience. Depending on the countries concerned and their previous situation, this is leading to changes in social and working relations not only within the schools themselves but also between them and the local authorities, taking the form either of greater dependence (France) or greater independence (England).

The identification of needs and investment planning

The aims of education policy and decisions on course options and curricula have to be translated into both quantitative and qualitative need for educational premises. The implementation of these objectives takes place within institutional frameworks which have been transformed by major shifts in the division of responsibility.

Planning of new buildings

A number of operations in the planning of educational building are being assigned to new authorities or shared with them: evaluation of existing accommodation capacities and their suitability; evaluation of the need for new buildings; decisions on their siting; choices between policies for the extension, renovation or modification of existing premises as against new construction; decisions on the opening and closure of schools; experiments in the reallocation of premises to other levels or types of education; and responsibility for maintenance programmes for existing buildings.

- In Greece, the powers of the Ministry of Education have been transferred to a public authority for educational building (OSK), which has responsibility for the planning, design, construction and equipping of school buildings in accordance with the Ministry's objectives. In this case by means of overall quantitative planning, the emphasis can be placed on consistency between the evaluation of existing accommodation capacities and new projects.
- In the Netherlands, in order to counteract the compartmentalisation of the various forms of educational provision, an integrated system for the overall planning of school building is envisaged (ROGO). This will be coordinated by the local authority concerned in consultation with central government for all decisions with budgetary implications. The main aim is to appraise and rationalise the use of existing and available premises (primary and secondary schools) before any new project is undertaken. Another aim is to give priority to the use of school buildings by the education system before any reallocation project goes ahead and to allow central government to facilitate transfers of premises between educational authorities.
- In France, educational planning at regional and local level has been extensively devolved and decentralised. It is currently split up into four phases: an outline forecast of course requirements, a forecast investment programme, plans detailing the educational structures of establishments and an annual schedule of operations. Responsibility for these phases is shared among several authorities: the local authority responsible for the establishment in question must secure the agreement of the other local authorities in whose area it will be sited and must seek the approval of central government, which allocates the teaching posts. Because of this diverse forms of cooperation between the services of the local and regional authorities and those of central government have developed in order to avoid the disparities which could result from conflicting aims.
- In Norway the municipalities are responsible for planning primary and lower-secondary education, including educational building, while the counties and their school boards are responsible for post-compulsory secondary education.

School closures

Decisions on the closure of schools are increasingly being devolved to the local level.

- In France decisions on closures, which in the first instance are governed by statutory enrolment thresholds, have been decentralised and made subject to joint decisions by the local authorities and the regional services of the Ministry.
- In Norway these decisions are the responsibility of the appropriate local authorities, which may also sell buildings even where their construction has been subsidised by central government.
- In England, however, decisions on closures or mergers are referred to the Department of Education and Science, following detailed discussions with the local community.

Responsibilities and methods of funding

The transfer of powers in the field of educational building has been accompanied by changes in sources and methods of funding, and in the sharing of burdens between national and local financing.

There have been changes in taxation arrangements and in the distribution of fiscal resources between the central and the regional and local authorities, as well as changes in systems of government grants to regional and local authorities, with the general trend being towards block grants and varying combinations of block and tied grants.

Capital expenditure allocations

- In France, funds equivalent to the amount that central government formerly spent on school building have been redistributed to the regional and local authorities. The resources previously earmarked for the building of primary schools have been incorporated within the block investment grant allocated to the communes. On the other hand, tied central government grants have been introduced for the *régions* and *départements* in accordance with new criteria and procedures for secondary school building. The Ministry also has responsibility for expenditure on educational equipment in line with decisions regarding curricula, over which it retains control.
- In Greece, funding resources have been shared since 1984 between the Ministry of Education and the regional authorities. The latter receive an overall central government grant, which they apportion to their various investment projects. Ownership of the buildings has been transferred to the communes in which they are sited.
- In Norway the regional or local authorities are responsible for funding as a whole. They can take out loans from a bank set up by the state if they cannot borrow enough locally. However, expenditure on the total running cost of secondary establishments is included in a block grant allocated by the state since 1986 to replace a variety of tied grants. It corresponds to the expenditure previously undertaken by the state in the various sectors covered by these tied grants. The local authorities are free to apportion this block grant as they see fit. There is in addition a tied central government grant for technical equipment. This is intended to cover initial equipment in line with the curricula for technical and vocational education: at least 40 per cent of the expenditure continues to be borne by the counties, apart from certain special fields where particularly costly equipment is eligible for up to 100 per cent grant. The state relies both on pressure from the users and on the interest of those responsible for policy at local level to maintain a scale of educational building expenditure consistent with requirements, while keeping down costs.
- In Portugal, educational building is now funded under cooperation agreements, between the Ministry of Education and the local authorities, which provide for joint financing. Between 10 and 30 per cent of the total cost is borne by the local authority and between 90 and 70 per cent by central government.
- In England, the breakdown between national and local tax resources works out to about half and half. Educational building is funded from a combination of local taxes (the Community Charge and Business Charge) and from government subsi-

dies (the Revenue Support Grant). This subsidy to the local authorities is essentially a block grant not tied to any specific educational purpose, but it is accompanied by recommendations for its use. In addition, some tied grants are made in order to encourage the local authorities to redeploy activities and expenditure in line with specific policies or priorities laid down by the Department of Education and Science (DES). The overall amount of the grant is fixed each year by the government in consultation with the associations of local authorities, the procedure being as follows:
   a) determination of the overall scale of requirements and local expenditure;
   b) determination of the proportion of this expenditure which will be covered by central government grants and the split between the block grant and tied grants;
   c) determination of the formula for allocating the block grant.
The government controls the overall amount of local authority expenditure by controlling the total amount of local authority borrowing (loan sanction). Within the overall framework laid down, local authorities are free to allocate their resources for whatever purpose they choose. Each local authority submits details of its educational building projects to the DES. The DES checks that the project is within the limits laid down for the authority for expenditure on education. The DES has also undertaken specific programmes outside the overall limits, for example to encourage work on energy saving or to remove asbestos from educational buildings.
 – In the Netherlands, control of funding remains highly centralised: the taxes involved are mainly those collected by the state. This situation has facilitated the development of a system for funding the construction and operation of primary schools. The purpose of this system is to make the most efficient use of money spent. Funding decisions, in each individual case, are analysed by taking into consideration all short and long-term costs. The system involves assembling and processing a vast range of information contained in a comprehensive database on the capital and operating costs of existing educational buildings. Although the system is an improvement on the traditional pragmatism in the planning of investment decisions, and at the same time maintains flexibility in the process, the task of keeping the database up-to-date proved more complex than had been envisaged, and some simplifications have had to be introduced.

Recurrent expenditure on buildings

The division of responsibility between the state and the regional and local authorities has changed in this area too.
 – For primary schools in the Netherlands a distinction is made between the structural costs of the building and costs arising from educational activity. Reductions are possible if, for example, one part of the premises remains unoccupied, and additions if, for example, additional premises outside the school are in use. The system thus makes it possible to refine forecasts and adjust budgets more in line with real costs.
 – In France the funds to cover the operating expenditure of the state on secondary schools at the time of devolution were reallocated to the regional and local authorities as part of a block grant, the *dotation générale de décentralisation*

(decentralisation block grant). The regional and local authorities themselves determine the amount of the funding for operating expenditure to be allocated to educational establishments under their control and the criteria for the distribution of the funds between establishments. These allocations replace the earlier Ministry of Education grants.
- In England the local authorities also determine their own systems for allocating funds for operating expenditure. These appropriations, however, must be approved by the DES. Management of funds is delegated to secondary and primary schools with over 200 pupils (and possibly also to smaller ones if the local authority deems it appropriate). The school is free to use the funds allocated to it as it sees fit: it may for example choose to recruit more teachers rather than to improve buildings.
- In Greece the communes are responsible for maintenance, upkeep and repairs. They receive funding from the regional authorities, who are in turn funded both by a block grant from the state and by allocations from the Ministry of Education.
- In Norway specific operating grants were phased out and replaced in 1986 by a block grant from the state to the regional and municipal authorities. This is calculated partly on the basis of criteria regarding educational needs. However it also includes a sectorial grant for establishments of upper secondary education, whereby the state funds almost half of the expenditure of these schools.

Responsibilities for design and construction

Generally, the regional and local authorities which own the buildings place contracts for works, appoint architects, undertake design studies and oversee building work. Educational suitability of the buildings has to be approved by the education authorities. Detailed physical and financial standards, designed in part to ensure a certain uniformity in the quality of educational building in each country, have been gradually applied less strictly and finally abandoned.
- In Norway the counties and municipalities own the buildings. They commission the work and appoint design offices and architects. There is a compulsory requirement of 11 square metres per pupil; however school plans and teaching programmes are no longer drawn up by the Ministry of Education, but by the counties. The Ministry now only intervenes in order to disseminate information.
- In France, since the enactment by law of "areas of responsibility", allocating to each category of authority the expenditure relating to a level of educational establishments, the *régions, départements* and *communes,* respectively, have been responsible for the construction, reconstruction, extension, major repair, equipping and physical operation of *lycées, collèges* and primary schools. However an authority other than the one which would normally be empowered to act may request responsibility in a particular case: thus a *commune* may take on the capital expenditure or physical operation of a *collège* or *lycée* instead of the *département* or *région* concerned, and would receive financial compensation in return.
- In England, the local education authorities (LEAs) are usually responsible for educational building. Programmes are drawn up either by their own architects' departments (these departments underwent considerable development in the 1960s and 1970s; some have recently become private organisations) or by private

architects. Construction is usually entrusted to private firms by competitive tendering.

The local authorities (or church authorities in the case of church schools) must submit proposals to the government for opening, extending or closing establishments. Detailed plans drawn up by the architects have to be approved by the educational building department of the DES. Space specifications and cost limits, which are understandable at a time of scarce resources and substantial demand, have been simplified in recent years. Individual projects were governed by national standards for the number of square metres per place and age of pupils and by costs per square metre. These standards were subsequently determined at local level, which has given rise to variations under the influence of both past experience of educational building and current building projects in other areas.

The influence exerted by the DES on the local authorities was particularly marked in the 1960s and 1970s, when school building activity and innovation in building methods were at their height. As a result, an extensive system of cooperation developed between the architects' department of the DES and those of the local authorities. However, this cooperation did not prevent major differences in cost-quality ratios. The slowdown in demand for new building has made it possible, within the context of this cooperation system, to devote more time to the planning of projects and to consideration of the need for maintenance.

- In Portugal, the construction of buildings for the first cycle of basic education is the responsibility of the municipalities. For the remainder of basic education and for secondary education, a cooperation agreement assigns to the municipalities the responsibility for acquiring and providing the site and preparing it for use (the acquisition of a site accounts for an increasingly large share of the total cost of the school, particularly in the larger towns).

The financial contribution of the municipality may also be provided in kind, with the work frequently being carried out by the municipal workforce and then quantified in expenditure terms. Although the majority of municipalities are ready and willing to assume their new responsibilities, many have limited technical capacity and few staff at their disposal. The danger is that such authorities may take on projects which they do not have the resources to complete. In many cases, therefore, they prefer to rely on the regional services of the state which already act as consultants for them.

Competitive tendering procedures are prepared at regional level on the basis of standard projects formulated at central government level, still following the pattern of former programmes. In 1990-91 four invitations to tender were put out simultaneously with differing specifications for each of the four regions of the country.

There is increasing consultation with the various groups and organisations concerned and future users (the school itself, parents' associations, neighbourhood groups, socio-educational associations, staff representatives).

- Norway places greater emphasis on consultation with future users and systematic assessments of buildings of a similar nature, particularly in the Scandinavian countries, than on regulations. In line with the new system of financing, the Ministry no longer issues instructions.
- In France the future school head has, in principle, to be appointed in advance so that he can participate in the planning of his school.

- In England the local authorities must demonstrate the demographic and educational justification and conformity to building regulations of their projects in the context of a public inquiry (lasting from 6 to 24 months). This obliges them to make informal approaches to the DES even during the planning phase.

In all the countries concerned maintenance is being given increasing priority. The funds allocated for maintenance are taking up a growing share of budgets compared with new construction, but the level of spending is not yet such that the building stock can be considered to be sufficiently well maintained. In many areas the situation is felt to be deteriorating and there is increasing concern in particular about the condition of the very large number of buildings put up in the 1960s and 1970s.

This priority, and the inadequacy of funds in relation to the obvious needs in this area, are prompting authorities to draw up programmes and schedules for maintenance and renovation operations, and to make arrangements for systematic action by qualified staff.

The day-to-day management of buildings

Institutional autonomy

Even countries which, unlike England or the Netherlands, do not have a long history of autonomy or "independence", have moved in the direction of granting a greater degree of autonomy to schools in the secondary sector. The scope of this freedom of action varies according to the country and area of operation concerned (educational, administrative or financial).

Every educational establishment, at least in the secondary sector, has its own board of governors. This body increasingly has the power to draw up, adopt and implement its budget. In such cases the school generally has a financial manager on its staff.

Governing bodies and administrators devote much of their time to the question of the maintenance and improvement of buildings. But often, through lack of funds or means of direct action, their procedure is to refer to higher authorities in order to alert them to the situation and ask them to carry out works which the schools do not have the resources to undertake themselves.

In recent years pupils' and parents' associations have more frequently been involved in the work of improving and decorating their schools.

- In France there is a system of *projets d'action éducative* (PAE) for the improvement of conditions in schools.

The landlord-tenant relationship

The traditional distinction between landlords' and tenants' liabilities is everywhere matched by a sharing of powers between local authorities (major works) and the institutions themselves (maintenance and minor work). Often, however, the distinction is an artificial and outmoded one and gives rise to unnecessary administrative work.

The technical vocabulary describing the various tasks of maintenance and upkeep is rich and varied and is not always precisely laid down, which gives rise to ambiguities in the apportionment of the various tasks. This division of work varies from one country to another, depending on a variety of criteria: the nature of the work, the sum involved, the size and the skills of the workforce assigned to the schools or technical services of the local authorities. It often seems ill-suited to ensuring the best use of teams of skilled workers and coordinated technical planning of maintenance work in the schools.

The budgets of educational establishments include amounts for maintenance and upkeep which are allocated either by the local or regional authorities responsible or by the Ministry of Education through its regional services, depending on the system of funding used.

Minor repairs are the responsibility of the education establishments and their heads. Their requests for more extensive work are financed by the local or regional authorities, generally at a level below the real need, out of appropriations and maintenance funds for public buildings as a whole.

The headteacher's freedom of action is restricted by certain rules limiting transfers from one budgetary item to another and by the group purchase schemes operated by some local authorities, in which their school may be required to participate, thus influencing or even imposing the choice of certain suppliers.

– In England the general rule now is that anything which does not come under the heading of major works (for which the local authorities, as owners of the buildings, are responsible) should be left to the schools themselves (in the past the local authorities looked after this work too).
– In France the *commune* decides on all maintenance and repair work in primary schools, whether it falls within the landlord's or tenant's responsibility. For secondary schools, the local and regional authorities take all decisions on matters falling within the scope of landlord liability. The authorities allocate funds to the schools to cover those operational and maintenance costs which are their responsibility. These grants are accompanied by guidelines for the use of the funds, which are implemented by the board of governors. The local or regional authority may also allocate tied grants to schools for more extensive work (repairs, extensions, improvements) for which it is responsible as landlord, thus taking decentralisation one step further.
– In Portugal, schools are responsible for maintenance, repairs and small-scale improvements. A fund maintained by the Ministry of Education has been set up in each school (in the second and third cycles of basic education and in secondary education) to cover the cost of routine work.
– In New Zealand, the Ministry of Education owns all school buildings and must maintain a complete inventory of them. This forms the basis of agreements on the assignment of buildings to the school governing boards, which are responsible for their management and maintenance and have the obligations of a tenant. This inventory also serves as the basis for the division of responsibilities between the Ministry of Education and the school, for the assessment of the grants necessary for routine maintenance and repair and for major works for which the Ministry is responsible.

Maintenance personnel

Depending on the country in question, the different types of work needed for the proper physical operation of educational establishments are carried out either by employees assigned to individual schools or groups of schools, by persons employed by the technical services of the local or regional authorities responsible or by outside firms supplying services on a commercial basis.

Depending on the level or amount of work involved, operations are performed by one or more of the employees assigned to the school, but these employees do not always have all the necessary skills. Where they do not, the work is carried out with outside assistance, either by workers belonging to the regional education services, by workers assigned to a group of schools or by workers employed by the local authority services.

- In Norway, for example, maintenance is generally performed by the county technical services.
- In France, by agreement between groups of schools, mobile teams of specialised workers (EMOP – équipes mobiles d'ouvriers professionnels) may be set up to carry out work according to a planned timetable in the various schools belonging to the group.
- In the Netherlands upkeep and repairs are carried out by staff employed by the school. Preventive maintenance, remedial maintenance and renovation work are carried out by outside specialists.
- In England the school head is now responsible for routine work and upkeep, but the upkeep of external spaces, external maintenance and repairs are carried out directly by a central service of the local authority. The personnel concerned thus fall under the authority of both the school head and the local authority service. Grant-maintained schools, which receive grants directly from the Department of Education and Science, do not receive the same technical support from the services of the local authorities. They will have to become more self-reliant and themselves hire the skilled staff they need (sometimes from their old local authority).
- In New Zealand, the local education administrations have reorganised themselves into service centres which are expected to be self-financing through the provision of services to schools, particularly in the field of maintenance. The schools, however, remain free to carry out the work themselves or to call in outside agencies.

Training

Increasing autonomy in matters concerning the construction, maintenance and management of buildings, as in other fields, is leading to a need for the provision and training of specialised staff, and hence to additional costs, potentially onerous for smaller schools.

This may in turn lead to the centralisation of certain functions within a main parent establishment or recourse to a service outside the schools themselves e.g. centralised accounting services and work-teams.

Greater responsibility for institutional and budgetary management also calls for higher standards in the recruitment and training of school heads.

Utilisation of the school for non-school activities

Most countries have sought to develop a number of integrated facilities which can be used for a variety of purposes, where the buildings have been specifically designed to have several functions. Not all the management problems of staffing, operating costs and their apportionment have been overcome.

All countries are seeking to make optimum use of the significant potential of educational premises for non-school activities. Requirements and motivations vary: adult continuing education, organisation of cultural, sporting, social or socio-educational activities on a non-profit-making basis and the general desire not to allow facilities as numerous and well-situated as school premises to be under-utilised, while at the same time having to build other facilities nearby to cater for the needs of the community.

Agreements are usually signed between the various parties concerned laying down the conditions under which buildings are to be used: duration of use, insurance, caretaking, cleaning, maintenance personnel. However, because of the nature of the organisations, often voluntary, which seek to make use of educational premises, the charges for their use are often symbolic and the proceeds are not sufficient to enable the school to cover the real costs, and frequently not even the marginal costs, arising from this additional use.

Effects and implications of recent changes

After 1945 the countries of Europe were confronted with an increase in demand for education, the result of which was a lengthening of the period of compulsory schooling, a massive increase in rates of enrolment and successive upsurges of demand for the continuation of studies beyond compulsory education. This made it necessary to undertake major building programmes and ensure an even distribution of the new buildings throughout a country.

The social priority and the magnitude assumed by the educational building sector of the construction industry, the volume of expenditure involved and its economic implications provided a justification for state intervention in planning, the central control of costs and construction projects, and standardization.

A huge stock of property was built up, mostly at a time when the cost of energy was not an overriding preoccupation: the increase in oil prices after 1974 therefore weighed heavily on the operating budgets of educational establishments, and energy saving programmes were introduced.

The need to build quickly and in quantity in order to meet the demand as it arose, together with constraints on public expenditure, gave rise to compromises, in the form of cost ceilings, between quantity and quality. This often resulted in shortcomings in quality and the choice of materials and techniques, creating a greater subsequent need for repairs and maintenance which has now become a major preoccupation in almost every country.

Once the bulk of this construction programme had been completed, quality requirements began to assume greater importance. The emphasis gradually shifted to such qualitative aspects as flexibility and adaptability to cater for pedagogical change; safety; comfort; energy saving; concern for the environment; and the modernisation of equipment.

At the same time a broader distribution of decision-making powers was sought in order to bring them closer to the users. This is seen in particular in the trend towards block grants, which has the effect of placing more of the initiative and responsibility at regional and local level.

However, new problems related to decentralisation are arising: changes in the pattern of central government involvement, the conditions and procedures for the assumption of their new powers by the local and regional authorities and educational establishments, compromises between capital projects in education and other priority investments, between new building and the renovation and improvement of the existing stock.

It is already possible to assess some of the effects of recent decisions and changes in the distribution of responsibilities on the scale and pattern of educational building.

The transfer of powers has been accompanied by debates on the state of the assets transferred, the amount of remedial work necessary, the scale of the operating costs generated and the apportionment of the resulting expenditure. The stock inherited by the new bodies responsible at regional and local level varies from one authority to another. Many consider that the state has done little but transfer the burden of costs without taking sufficient account of real needs or of the great disparities between regions which have been inherited from the past. Fears are expressed about the risks of imbalance between transfers of powers and transfers of costs, and the danger that regional disparities may be exacerbated.

The maintenance by the state of systems of block or tied grants is being accompanied by a questioning of the data on which these grants are based and the methods by which they are calculated.

The transferring of powers, seen against the background of the situation in each country, is designed to create a more rational balance between the responsibilities of central government, the two or three levels of local government and the educational establishments themselves. The overriding trend, however, is in the direction of devolution, decentralisation and increased autonomy for the schools.

But trends in the opposite direction may be observed in countries where traditionally there has been a high degree of local autonomy.

- In England, for example, the effect of the 1988 Education Act is to strengthen the autonomy of educational establishments *vis-à-vis* the local authorities and at the same time to increase the scope for centralisation, e.g. the introduction of a national curriculum and the possibility for a school with more than 300 pupils to decide to be dependent for its funding on the Department of Education and Science rather than on the local authorities.

  If a large number of these schools choose this alternative, the result could be an imbalance in restructuring, refurbishment and maintenance policies, depending on whether or not the schools are covered by national funding and programmes.

  Thus, at both local and national levels, a re-ordering of priorities is taking place. However, the acquisition by the regional and local authorities of greater responsibility for the property inventory and for educational building, bringing these responsibilities closer to the users, has been coupled with a greater degree of block funding.

- In France, despite initial fears, it would seem that overall funding for secondary school building has not suffered as a result of decentralisation – quite the con-

trary. The regional and local authorities have assumed their new responsibilities and have allocated from their own resources additional funds to educational building over and above the grants received.
– In Norway the replacement of tied grants by a block grant seems also to have been accompanied by an increase in the educational expenditure of the regional and local authorities, due primarily to the increase in the number of teaching posts.

In all cases transfers of power have been accompanied by new working relationships, calling for increased coordination between central and local government, school heads and other organised groups (churches in the case of the Netherlands and England, teachers' unions and parents' associations).
– In the Netherlands, the effectiveness of the new system depends on cooperation between the administrators of the system, local authorities and school heads. Only this cooperation makes it possible both to take full advantage of the system and the wealth of information and experience it can digest and evaluate, and to avoid falling prey to excessive concern for cost-cutting at the expense of quality and long-term considerations.
– In France, the 1983 Education Act set up a system of power-sharing between several authorities. Because of this, in many regions various forms of cooperation between the services of the local authorities and those of central government have emerged as a way of avoiding the inconsistencies which could result from conflicts of opinion, for example, the desire of an authority to build a school which, because it is not deemed to be a priority by the Ministry of Education, would not be allocated the necessary teaching posts in time.

In the design and construction of educational buildings, emphasis is placed in all countries on consultation with those who will eventually be responsible for and have the use of the building.

School autonomy generally makes for greater flexibility and speed in decision-making regarding premises, better adjustment to needs and more effective exercise by the community of its responsibilities because of its closeness to the decision-making centre. Autonomy and the development of multiple uses for premises (sports facilities as well as school buildings) will only work however if there is constant cooperation between those concerned.

The new division of powers and funding responsibilities has had effects, depending on the extent of a region's financial capacity and its choice of priorities, on regional disparities in the availability of equipment, the scale and quality of educational building and the way in which buildings are used.

Bearing in mind the recentness of some of these developments in policy and legislation, these effects cannot always be clearly discerned. They may in the future necessitate policies on the part of the state to compensate for these disparities and the maintenance of, or an increase in, the proportion of grant aid, thereby making it possible to exert more influence on local decisions.

Local autonomy, at the level of both the educational establishment and the regional or local authority, by bringing the powers of decision-making and funding closer to the users, may enhance the efficiency and responsiveness of management but it may also make certain measures to rationalise the school network more difficult, particularly decisions on school closures.

Decentralisation may be hindered by fears the schools may have, that, although they themselves enjoy greater freedom of action, the regional and local authorities will be granted more powers with respect to them.

Today we are seeing the results of the major building programmes undertaken during the period of growth in the school-age population (and particularly the use of industrialised building systems) in the form of substantial needs for renovation, maintenance and refurbishment.

The importance of maintenance was for a long time overlooked because of the need for new building to keep pace with the additional intake, which always carried priority in public opinion, and cost constraints which led to allocations of funds being set at levels below estimated requirements. The state of the existing building stock has deteriorated. In the choice of materials and energy systems, sufficient account was not always taken of the operating costs they would generate.

Buildings may also impose added maintenance requirements because of over-utilisation as the result of the increasing tendency to make educational premises available to other users, of overcrowding, deterioration in certain problem areas of cities and inadequate maintenance programmes in the interval between major renovations.

Even where there has been decentralisation, it is arguable that certain powers with regard to decision-making and funding, and technical and consultancy services should be retained or even established at central government level. However the policy of decentralisation has generally prevailed, thus reducing the powers of central government departments and services (Norway, France), but various bodies have been set up or maintained with certain changes in their functions:

a) In the ministries themselves:
- In England the Department of Education and Science maintains an Architects and Buildings Branch.
- In France a central body, the central advisory service for the regional and local authorities (CCTCT – Centre de Conseil Technique aux Collectivités Territoriales), was retained after decentralisation. Its function was to serve as a resource centre and to compile technical manuals and reference documents, which were not compulsory but were in fact extensively used. Even so, this body was wound up at the end of 1989.
- In New Zealand, the new Ministry of Education includes a property management unit whose job is to oversee work carried out on property belonging to the state, prepare agreements on the use of buildings by educational establishments, operate a system of property data bases, define standards and offer technical advice to schools.

b) In inter-state or inter-regional bodies:
- In the former Federal Republic of Germany, the Conference of Ministers of Education, a body for cooperation between the Länder, which are responsible for education policy, has set up a Centre for Standards and Efficiency in Educational Affairs whose task is to prepare recommendations to the Länder and local and district authorities on matters of educational building, conduct and coordinate research projects, develop and disseminate specialised documentation and provide advisory services. A recent project sets out, on the

basis of national and foreign case studies on the renovation and rehabilitation of educational buildings, to compile a list of items and criteria for the evaluation of the potential use of buildings.
c) In independent research institutes or agencies:
- The Netherlands has a school building information centre which is an independent non-profit-making body.

More efficient management of resources is everywhere a major concern.

a) At the level of the local authorities responsible for educational establishments efforts are being made to:
- Develop global approaches to the improvement and management of an authority's entire educational building stock, covering all the successive phases: construction, installation, maintenance, and use;
- Diversify sources of funding: central government grants but also the authorities' own resources and borrowings; incentives to identify instances of under-utilisation together with the option of proposing to the owner, the state, that part of the site or premises surplus to requirements be sold off with a view to improving the rest of the property (New Zealand);
- Refine the criteria for the allocation of operating funds to schools;
- Promote the idea of requiring each school to pay a rental charge per square metre (or at least to calculate and communicate a figure for this to the school) in order to encourage more rational use of premises (in Norway some counties are considering this).

b) At the level of the educational establishments themselves the following are being considered:
- The formulation of upkeep and maintenance schedules in order to develop an overall approach to the physical management of all of the premises belonging to a school;
- The possibility of allowing autonomous educational establishments the right to retain the savings resulting from prudent management of premises and funds;
- Multipurpose use of school buildings.

Generally speaking, the attempt to improve the way in which premises are managed and used must not obscure their primary purposes; it is a question not of the lowest cost but of the best cost/benefit ratio, and indicators of management efficiency need to be considered in conjunction with indicators of the social and educational quality of these premises, based on thorough and up-to-date knowledge not only of construction and operating costs, but also of the ways in which educational buildings are actually used.

Diagrams of Education Systems

General Observations

These diagrams give an outline of the structure of the regular education systems in the five countries. Only the most common types of education, internal flows and outflows are indicated. Similarly, neither the inflows of adults into third level education, which vary in magnitude from country, nor the types of education specially designed for them are shown.

The size of the boxes is in no way proportionnal to the number of pupils/students concerned

The duration indicated for a particular type of education is that which applies in the majority of cases: it may differ for certain fields of study, particularly in third level or part–time education.

The ages indicated for the different levels of education apply to pupils/students whose passage through the system has followed the normal pattern, i.e. to those who have neither been kept back nor moved up and who have not interrupted their studies, particularly prior to enrolment in third level education.

Pre-primary education has been coupled with primary education although, depending on the country concerned, it may be provided either in sections attached to primary schools, in separate establishments, or in both.

FRANCE

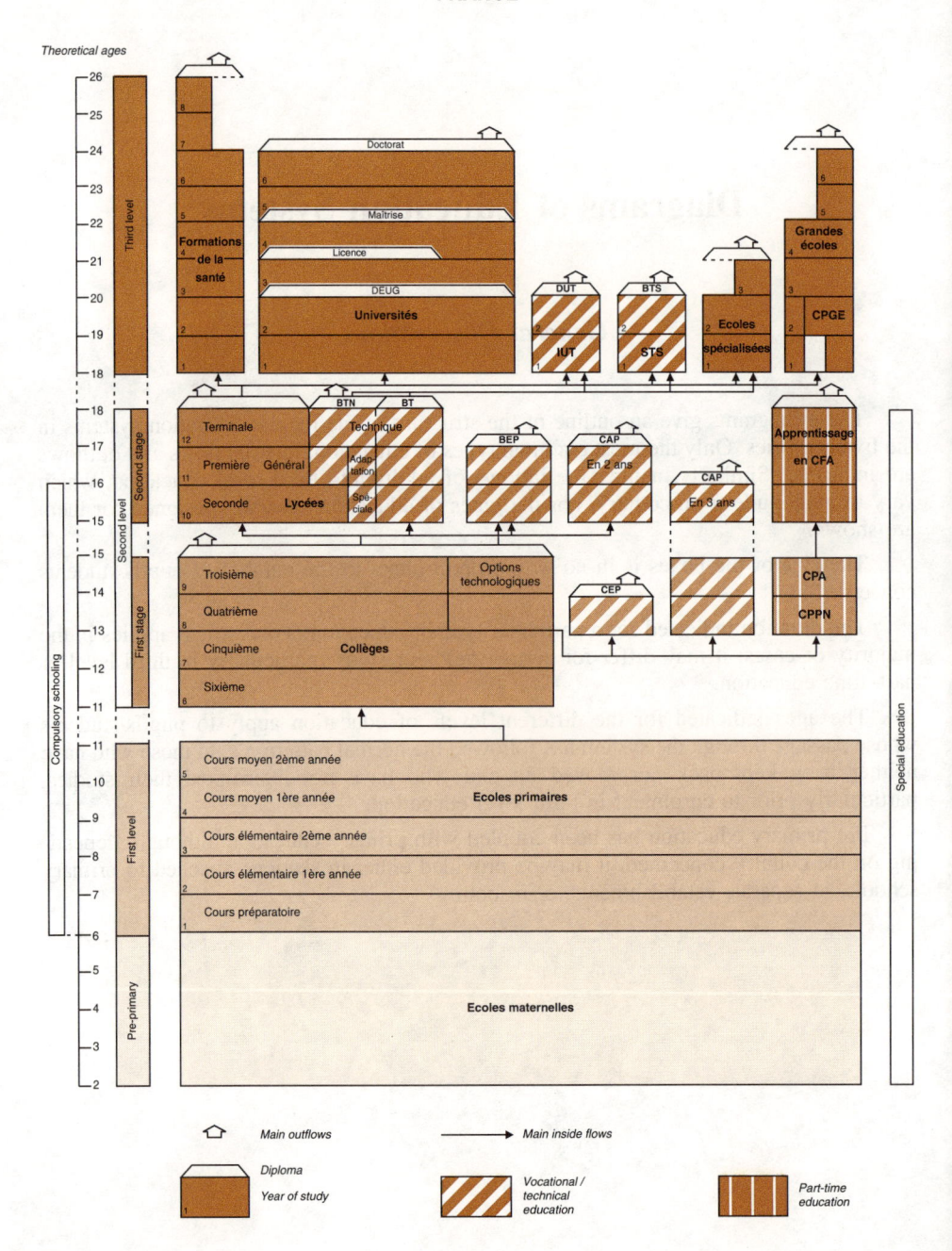

THE NETHERLANDS
Full-time education only

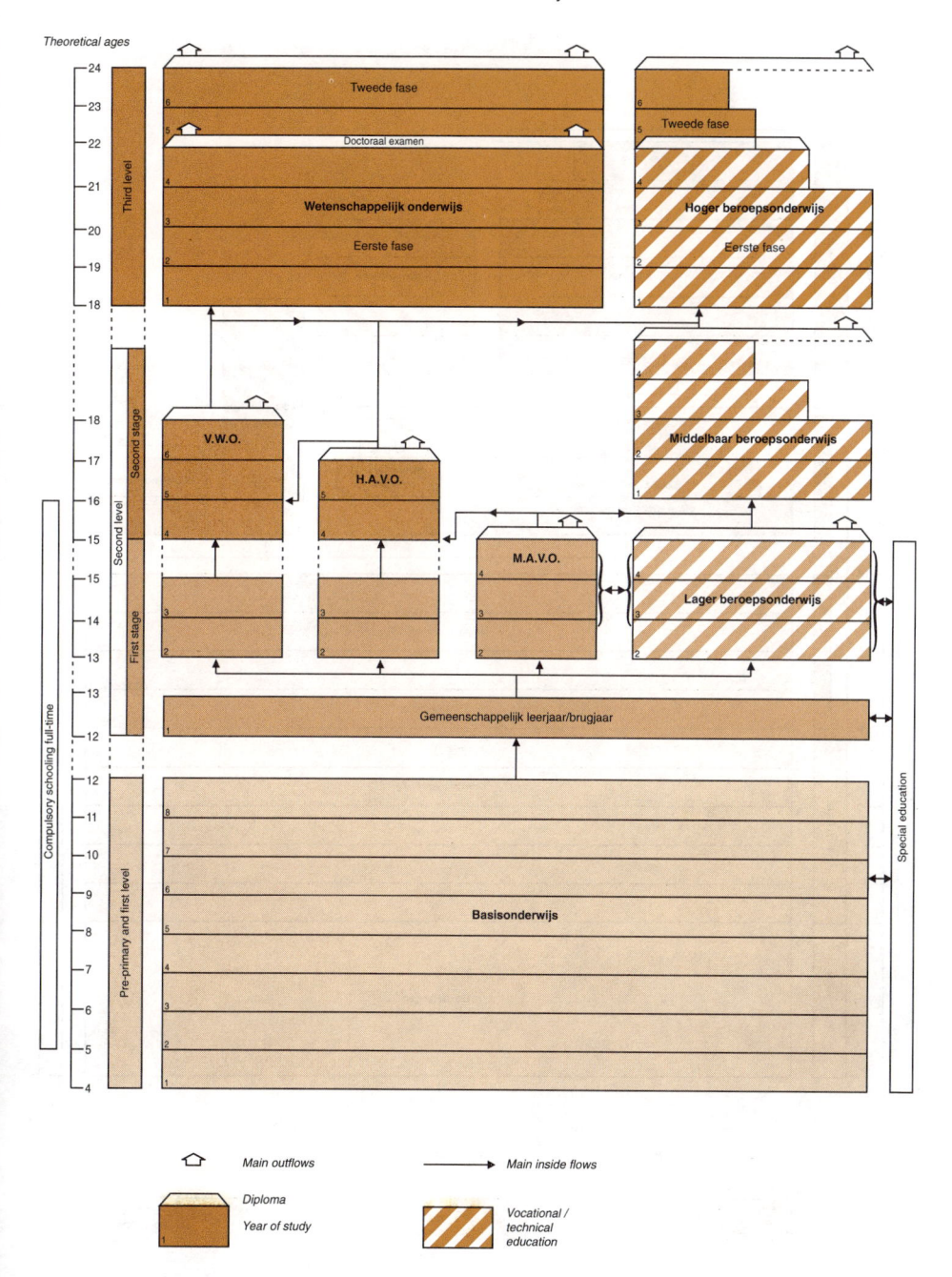

Theoretical ages

Third level
- Tweede fase
- Doctoraal examen
- Wetenschappelijk onderwijs
- Eerste fase
- Tweede fase
- Hoger beroepsonderwijs
- Eerste fase

Second level

Second stage
- V.W.O.
- H.A.V.O.
- Middelbaar beroepsonderwijs

First stage
- M.A.V.O.
- Lager beroepsonderwijs
- Gemeenschappelijk leerjaar/brugjaar

Pre-primary and first level
- Basisonderwijs

Compulsory schooling full-time

Special education

Legend:
- ⬆ Main outflows
- → Main inside flows
- Diploma
- Year of study
- Vocational / technical education

Note : Full-time compulsory schooling is followed by one year of part-time compulsory schooling.

NORWAY

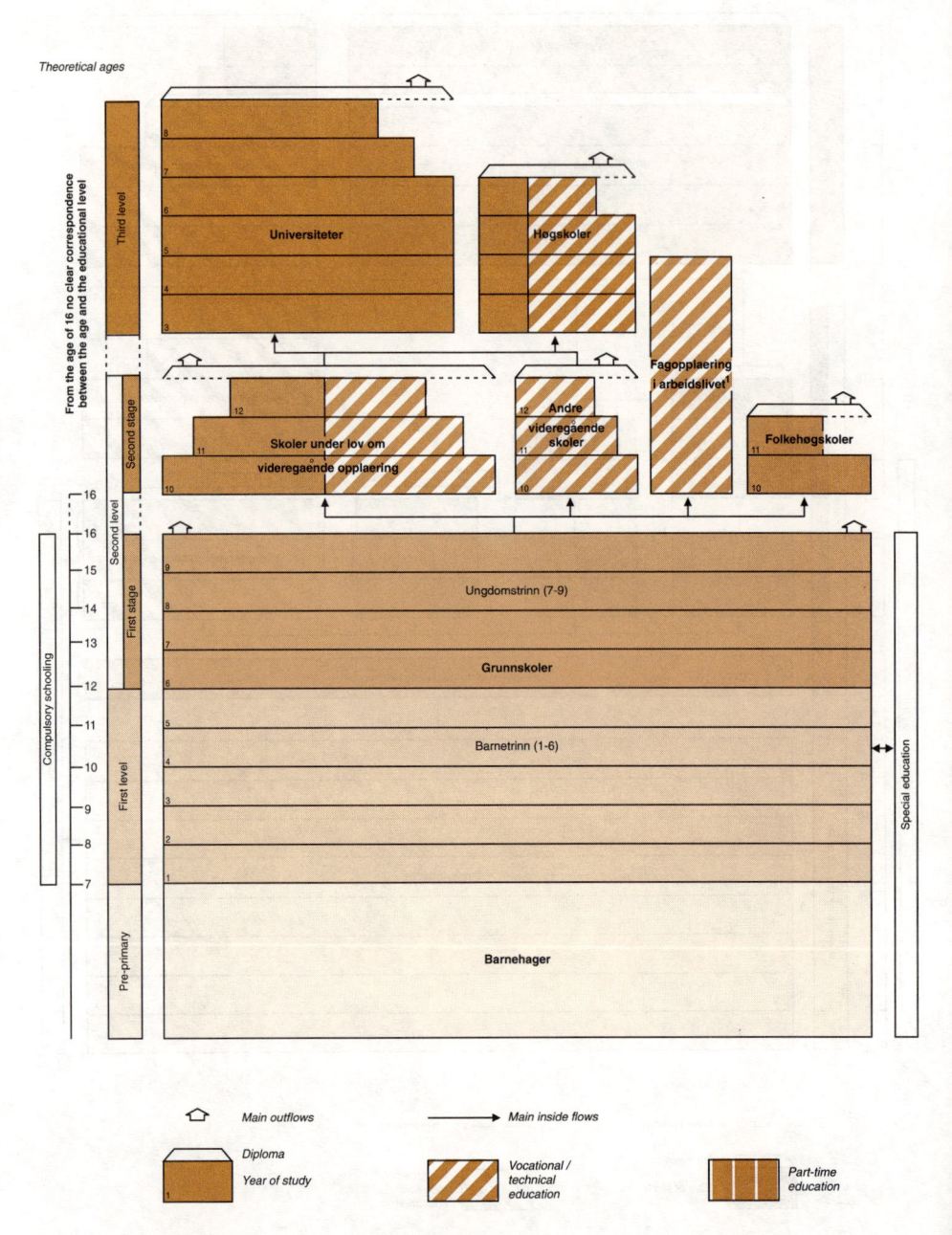

1. Systematic training in the world of work (i. e. apprenticeship 3 - 5 years).

PORTUGAL

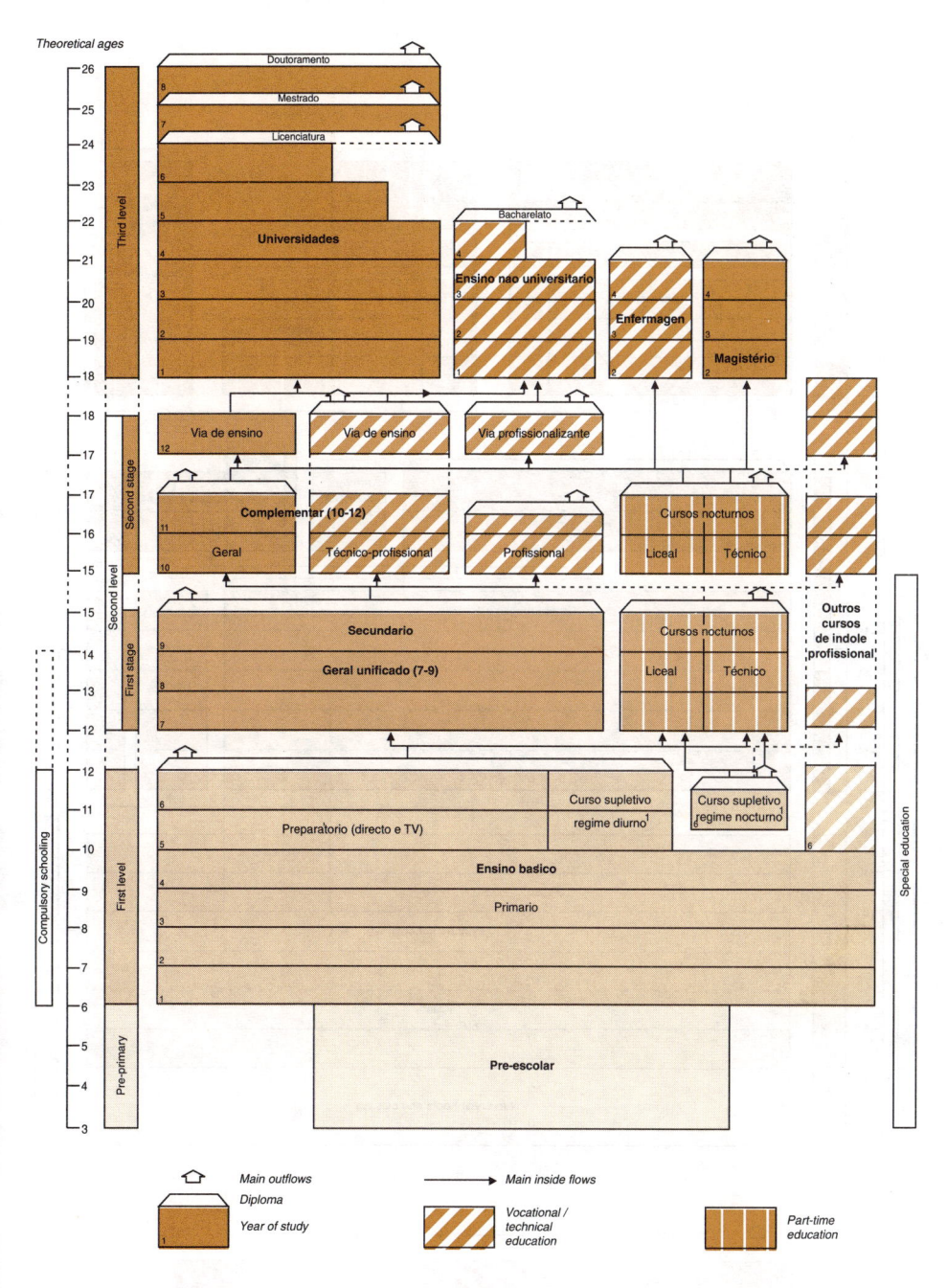

1. For young people 14-18 years old to complete basic education. Day courses for those not working and evening courses for workers.

UNITED KINGDOM   ENGLAND AND WALES
The education system is somewhat different in Scotland and in Northern Ireland

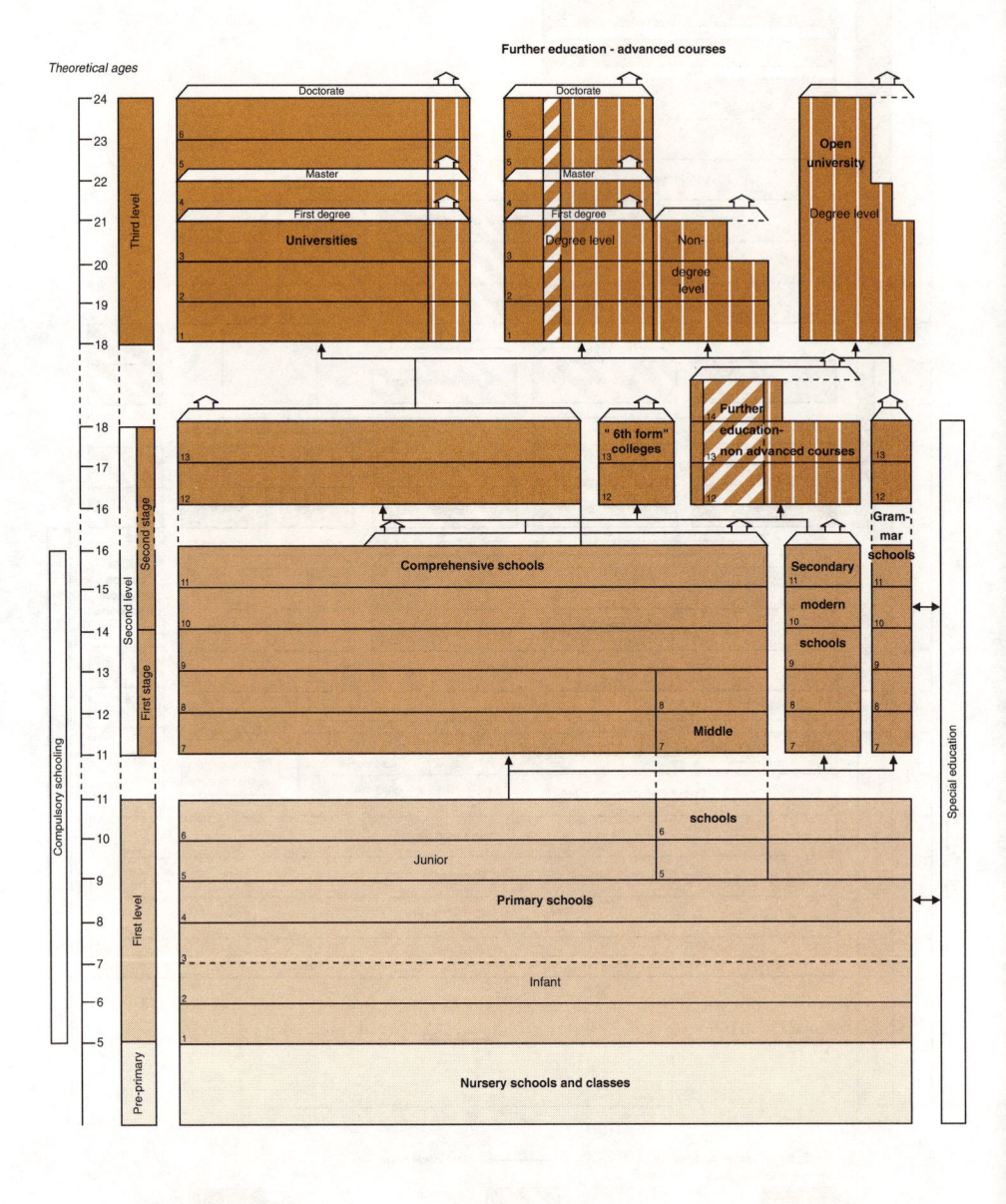

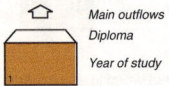

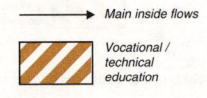

Conference Conclusions

Starting from the very different situations presented, and the comparison of the effects of recent changes and developments, conference participants observed a broad trend towards decision-making processes which are more decentralised, that is, closer to the users of the service. They felt that in general terms this process of "decentralisation" could lead to more effective management of buildings. They warned, however, that decentralised management should not be seen as a panacea, and that it was not a substitute for adequate levels of funding. Where maintenance backlogs had been allowed to build up, for example, it was still necessary for resources to be made available to reduce them.

Having said that, they felt it preferable not to try to define "decentralisation" in ideal terms. The word is loaded with divergent meanings, and applied to many specific sets of circumstances which arise from the history, politics and culture of the countries concerned. It is more worthwhile to analyse in each case the conditions for coherent sharing of responsibility between different authorities, and their medium and long-term implications.

As well as historical, cultural and constitutional factors, the area of activity in question, and the size of the country concerned, will influence the choice of central or local control. In a small country, where the total population may be less than than in a single region of a larger one, central administration can be close to local level and there is little need for intermediate layers of authority. Usually, however, one can identify a central level, the level of the institution, and one or more intermediate administrative levels, all cooperating in the implementation of decisions which are necessarily shared.

Participants tried to identify which elements in the process of providing and running educational buildings should remain centralised, or at least coordinated at national or inter-regional level; and how to ensure the coordination necessary for planning, financing, construction, building management, maintenance, management of technical staff, and the conditions and priorities for the use of buildings.

The decision-making process itself is a network of complicated and inter-related decisions taken by a number of distinct authorities - but the assessment of the optimum level for a given type of decision is a matter for each country. Choices about the sharing of powers depend also on the degree of development of the educational system and on the availability of a sufficient number of trained personnel on the staff of the authorities which will exercise new powers.

Participants noted that authorities, at whatever level, have often made considerable efforts to meet new demands for school buildings, undertaking massive building programmes in short periods of time, but that few appear to be able consistently to provide the resources necessary to maintain the stock of schools adequately. Moreover, when demand for education is increasing rapidly, there is always a danger that the need to provide new places will override consideration of the long-term maintenance problem created by initial shortcomings in design and construction. Centralised planning, which permits quick and economical construction on a large scale, using standardized plans and methods, has led to a situation in which, in some areas, a very large number of buildings are reaching the end of their useful lives at the same time, and will create a demand for renovation and replacement which threatens to far outstrip the resources available.

In this context there was some discussion about the aim of decentralisation. It is usually justified on one of two grounds. Either efficiency – a more locally based system is likely to be more responsive to needs, and more efficient in the allocation of resources; or democracy – it is right to give the users of the educational system a greater say in its management. Both these arguments were seen to have some weight, but some feared that decentralisation masked an attempt to pass on the burden of maintaining an increasingly expensive building stock from central to local authorities.

The sacrifice of long-term maintenance to short-term quantitative needs did not however appear inevitable to participants, and they concluded that it would be worthwhile seeking ways to transfer experience of long-term cost planning (life-cycle costing) from those countries which have applied it to educational buildings and which no longer have large programmes of new building, to those which are having to cope with a rapid increase in demand.

Central functions

It was felt that in general central authorities should:
- Define a policy which sets out the broad aims of education;
- Forecast total pupil numbers, including those arising from inter-regional population movement, and evaluate the corresponding need for places;
- Oversee the quality and the suitability of the building stock;
- Determine the initial distribution of resources between services (e.g. education) and to some extent within services (e.g. for the maintenance and development of the building stock);
- Establish, and maintain for as long as is necessary, policies which compensate for regional inequalities;
- Define minimum quality standards – these can be more or less detailed, and must always be justified. It is for discussion how they should be stated and implemented, what safeguards they should include and how to check that they are applied. Advice and guidance is to be preferred to statutory control where possible;
- Set staffing standards;
- Monitor overall quality and outcomes;
- Organise pilot projects;
- Carry out, or ensure that others carry out, necessary research, both for scientific/technical as well as managerial reasons;
- Create and maintain data-bases which are accessible, so that "the wheel does not have to be reinvented".

Functions to be carried out at a more local level

The remaining tasks of planning and management can be devolved to local level. This level could be that of the institution or of the local authority. The size of the school is an important element in deciding what functions can be delegated. Whatever the case it must be remembered that the essential task of the head, or principal, is to ensure educational quality. Preoccupation with other tasks must not distract him from this fundamental one. There is therefore a need for a category of qualified, or trained, staff to deal with the management of property on behalf of the institution.

A distinction has to be drawn between single-service local authorities, responsible solely for education, and multiple-service local authorities, responsible additionally for some aspects of social services, health care, housing and roads. Multiple-service authorities are particularly well placed to take a role in property management.

So far as the maintenance and day-to-day running of buildings is concerned, one simple principle is widely accepted: minor maintenance and repairs should be carried out at the level of the school. Major maintenance is the responsibility of a more aggregated level where specialists can serve a large number of establishments.

Decisions about the rationalisation of the network of educational buildings in a given locality – restructuring, amalgamation, closure, sale of disused or under-utilised property – are constrained by the geographical, as well as the local political and "psychological", context. They must be based on forecasts and technical formulae, but they demand first a philosophy, or overall concept, of the need for and the means of this rationalisation, and its corresponding benefits. This overall concept must be shared by the majority of local politicians, by the public, and by the bodies which represent it.

Such decisions about rationalisation will only be reached if the advantages of difficult measures can be seen locally, and in the short term, and if it can be clearly seen that they do not damage the quality of the education available.

Bringing decision-making responsibility to a more local level has the following advantages:
- More account can be taken of local characteristics in building;
- Users of buildings can develop a sense of ownership. This in turn can lead to greater awareness of the need to look after the buildings and to a reduction in vandalism. Some convincing experiences were described by participants, including contracts made with pupils to maintain the condition of the facilities they use, based on a clear understanding of the implications of financial damage for the school. Such contracts seem to have the effect of reducing damage;
- The effectiveness of budgetary decisions can be improved, since local politicians have a better understanding of local priorities.

It has to be accepted however that local responsibility means what it says. There may be:
- A more or less wide variation in quality standards;
- A reduction in some areas, or an increase in others, of the resources devoted to educational buildings if other priorities are identified locally;
- Greater complexity and length in the planning process.

Care has to be taken not to create a system which is unduly complex. A decentralised system will be characterised by negotiations and discussions between different groups and levels, rather than by norms and dictats from the centre. Efforts must be made to keep the procedures as simple as is possible.

Requirements of decentralised systems

The fundamental process in the management of any educational system is the distribution of resources. The central authority must be responsible, at national level, for the initial "division of the cake" and for ensuring that the total amounts available are adequate. Beyond this decisions need to be taken on the degree of specificity attached to the allocations made to local authorities, or to individual institutions. A block grant or lump sum covering a number of services gives more discretion to the local level to make choices about funding, and thus weakens the ability of the central authority to control outcomes in detail. Specific grants will be used by the central authority to protect certain categories of expenditure, or to promote new policies.

In very decentralised systems safeguards must be established. Where local democracy and decision-making is developing, these safeguards need less and less to take the form of obligations. This is not a question of following strict and detailed rules but rather of being able to seek advice, which should be available from experienced individuals and organisations.

One important task is to respond to the requirement for availability and exchange of information which is created by decentralisation: professionals, administrators, politicians and the public are all involved in their own way in the success of projects. They need up-to-date and coherent information adapted to their interests and responsibilities.

It seems appropriate, in particular, to maintain or to create at a national level (or at some other central coordinating level) organisations for research, advice and information. Their status (more or less dependent on the state or local authorities) and their role can vary, according to the country, from simple advice and information exchange to a more interventionist one *vis-à-vis* local authorities which are developing their own school building services.

It is necessary to coordinate central and local research and advisory efforts. The role of these bodies is also to contribute to the international exchange of information and to disseminate it within the country. In this way, countries confronted with urgent quantitative needs and with limited budgets, and which have not been able to carry out their own research, can benefit from the experience of others.

The availability of well-trained staff in sufficient numbers to constitute a pool of expertise to resolve local problems without having to call on higher-level authorities is an essential condition for effective decentralisation. The degree of decentralisation possible is a function of the qualifications and aptitude of the authority or institution concerned to assume the tasks entrusted to it. If they are weak, training will need to be given and for a while more detailed guidance may be necessary.

Training and information adapted to the needs of those involved in the process of building can also promote changes in attitudes and behaviour, which are necessary for more decentralised planning and more autonomous management. They should also aim at raising the awareness of the public – and in particular of teaching and non-teaching staff, and pupils – of the buildings.

In conclusion

The changes which have taken place in different national and local circumstances, in the planning, financing and management of educational buildings can be considered from the three viewpoints of efficiency, equity and quality and in the light of the effect they have on construction, improvement, management, maintenance and the overall service offered to the public.

In the search for quality and effectiveness, authorities of different levels form a whole. Autonomy, just like the exercise of central power which respects that autonomy, has to be learned, particularly in situations where they represent a break with a long tradition.

When roles change old reflexes often remain. Central authorities may wish, or may be suspected of wishing, to recover through an information system the decision-making powers which they have had to transfer to another level, even if this was done for reasons of efficiency, equity or quality.

The local authority or establishment which has been given responsibility for decisions can be inhibited in exercising it by the absence of experienced staff or by the lack of knowledge of similar experience elsewhere, and thus be in need of advice. If this responsibility is to be accepted and is not to create dependence anew, it must be presented as an offer of help and not as an obligatory consultation or approval.

Dependence may persist if the local authority continues to seek approval for decisions which it is competent to take itself.

In every situation it is necessary to maintain a balance between overall policy and the encouragement of centres of responsibility which are closer to the users and which take more account of local circumstances.

The advantages brought about by a better articulation of the entire planning and financing process in educational building, and by a distribution of power which gives all those involved a sense of their own responsibility, can be demonstrated by the example of energy conservation. Many decisions at different levels have to be coordinated: they cover financial help to enable new buildings to incorporate energy-saving measures; research; pilot projects and the dissemination of results; the need to take account of local climatic conditions in design; funding of "first-aid" measures for existing buildings; training and awareness programmes for heads and their staff about the savings which can be realised by simple actions; and the implementation of these actions by a large number of individual building users. All these elements together produce increased efficiency and savings which can be used for other educational purposes. The same should be true of new systems for the overall planning and management of educational buildings.

Note on Central and Eastern Europe

At the invitation of the Netherlands Ministry of Education and Science, Hungary, Poland and the Czech and Slovak Federal Republic (CSFR) sent observers to the conference. Radical changes have recently been taking place in these countries, leading to the development of democratic governments based on a multi-party system, which are working towards the introduction of a market economy. Constitutional reform and the election of new presidents are the principal elements in this process which have taken place to date, setting the tone for further change. Such changes are taking place in all areas of life, including education. It will be easier to shape and implement the processes of change if use can be made of the knowledge and experience acquired by other countries which have for many years enjoyed the conditions to which Eastern European countries aspire. It was in order to exchange knowledge and experience in this way that the invitation was made.

Comments and responses received after the conference indicate that the degree to which changes have taken place varies from country to country. The same may be said of the objectives pursued by each country.

A number of countries are still engaged in studying what form education and the relationship between schools and central and local government should take so as to meet the new demands being imposed by society. Others, notably the CSFR, have completed that stage and are now deciding on the steps to be taken. Planning, state funding and – in a market economy – other sources of finance for school buildings, are on the agenda at this stage.

The value of the conference for this process is analysed below.

It should be noted that all the observers emphasized the importance of participation in the conference and the exchange of knowledge which took place. They proposed that contacts be further developed.

No sooner is one question answered than another arises. For this reason, the observer countries would like to see more analysis of the procedures and systems employed in Western Europe, both on the basis of current and future reports and notes on the conference, and through the continuation, wherever possible, of direct links. The aim is to find or develop methods, procedures, systems, formulae and regulations which are appropriate to local conditions and which meet local requirements.

One of the CSFR observers, noting that the CSFR stands on the threshold of a process of radical, long-term change, emphasised the need for knowledge and experience. Accordingly, the observer produced a provisional report on the conference and discussed it with the Deputy Minister responsible for school buildings. The results of these talks have been incorporated in decision-making on the organisation of schools. A report summarising the information required is being drawn up.

It has not proved easy to put changes into effect while according due weight to the historic context. Municipalities which traditionally had rights and responsibilities of their own were, so to speak, swallowed up by central government more than 40 years ago. It will take a long time for them to regain their autonomy.

New legislation on the organisation of education, which entered into force in December 1990, is therefore of a temporary nature. Responsibility in most fields still rests with central government or with district school authorities set up by the Ministry of Education. The goal is to evaluate this legislation in a few years and then divide responsibilities between the Ministry and autonomous school boards in a more balanced way.

Part Two

CONFERENCE PAPERS

Welcoming address

Mr.dr.ir. J.M.M. Ritzen, Minister of Education and Science

It gives me great pleasure to welcome participants, and especially our guests from the CSFR, Hungary and Poland, to this conference.

The development of the relationship between the OECD and the countries of Central and Eastern Europe has been given added impetus by the political changes which took place in those countries in 1989. The invitations to Hungary, Poland and the CSFR to send Observers to this Conference underline the importance which both the OECD and the Dutch Government attach to the strengthening of relations and the exchange of knowledge with these countries.

One of PEB's objectives is to promote the exchange of knowledge and views on all aspects of educational building. The theme of this conference, the planning and funding of educational building, is a very topical one, not only in the Netherlands but in many other countries, as is illustrated by the high level of participation.

The balance between central and local responsibilities differs greatly from country to country. When the Dutch Government took office last November, I followed the turn-around started by my predecessor in which the objective was no longer decentralisation in general, bringing power from central governments to decentralised governments, but rather bringing power from central governments to individual schools: increased autonomy for schools.

The new Government intends to reduce the role of central government to a number of core tasks. In the past, the Government has assumed responsibility for many matters which, for various reasons, were receiving too little attention. This means that the Government now performs many tasks which could also be done often more efficiently by those directly involved. The idea is not that the Government should relinquish all responsibility for these matters but that it should limit itself to setting targets, taking into account the interests of society as a whole, and to ensuring that targets are met.

The core tasks of government with respect to education include guaranteeing the quality of education, and ensuring that pupils receive equal educational opportunities, irrespective of their social or ethnic background. In the Netherlands, as in other countries, if we are to guarantee the quality of our education system, it is important that we seek to enhance the social status of teachers and improve the organisation of schools by achieving an optimum size and ensuring professional management. These core tasks must then be funded within existing education budgets. It is very difficult to get politicians to find new funds for increasing the education budget. Funds must be released elsewhere if an improvement in quality is to be achieved. One option is to create larger schools which would achieve two objectives: they would probably be closer to an optimum size in educational terms, and would possibly offer a better basis for management.

The aim of policy remains more cost-effective financial management with funding systems which are simple, clear and manageable. Schools and institutions which are responsible for the educational process need continuity of funding from central government in order to plan ahead efficiently.

The decentralisation of school management forces government to plan its budget carefully so as to avoid short-term emergency measures. This gives rise to the need for manageable funding systems and reliable information on which budget estimates can be based. An important instrument for the decentralisation of school management, on the one hand, and good budget management on the other, is funding formulas. A large number of funding formulas have been put forward in the Netherlands. These are based on principles of simplicity – both of the system itself and of its application – justice, and cost-effectiveness. The size of the institution is then a very relevant factor. A primary school with an annual budget of say two hundred thousand guilders (one hundred thousand dollars approximately) will require a more specific system of allocating funds than a university with a budget of 320 million guilders (160 million dollars approximately). This implies different funding formulas for schools with different sizes.

For universities, it is our aim to create a very simple system of output funding, whereby the block grant is allocated on the basis of the number of students who pass their examinations, i.e. on the basis of the product delivered. The institutions themselves are then authorised to take decisions on investments which are funded by that annual block grant. But such a system can only be applied when the institution is of a sufficiently large size.

I would like to draw your attention to a draft framework agreement which I recently drew up in consultation with colleges of higher vocational education. A similar agreement is being drawn up now for universities. These agreements, which have to be approved by Parliament and by the organisations representing the colleges and universities, are a significant example of the Government's decision to adopt a "hands-off" approach to education and reduce the use of statutory instruments, and they are relevant to the subject of this conference.

Under the agreements, responsibility for the planning side of accommodation will gradually be transferred to the institutions themselves. These institutions will be empowered, in the long run, to take decisions on investment; this goes together with the provisional decision to provide annual block grants for investment financed by commercial loans taken out by the institutions. To enable this the Government and the institutions must draw up regulations which remove existing impediments and lay the budgetary foundations for increased autonomy. These impediments relate to the operation of the institutions on the capital market and the fact that central government has at present a claim on all buildings and sites on the basis of their funding under the regulations currently in force. We call that claim economic ownership, and it means, among other things, that property may not be sold or mortgaged and that the profits from the disuse or sale of sites or buildings must be turned over to central government. Under the new system, economic ownership would be transferred from government to colleges and universities to provide them with the means to maintain their accommodation independently. This is not yet reality but we are working towards it. In the area of senior secondary vocational education we are working in the same direction. This has been made possible by a large scale merger operation which brought average annual school budgets to between 10 million and 15 million guilders. However, the smaller the school budget the greater must be the degree of detail in the funding formula; this applies in our country more specifically to secondary and primary schools. In these sectors funding systems are required which take into account the specific features of the school so that their grant corresponds directly to expenditure, assuming sober and cost-effective management.

Resource Allocation and Educational Quality

A.M.L. van Wieringen

How can a resource allocation system which concerns itself with buildings and equipment be explicitly directed at aspects of education likely to improve quality?

In order to answer that question it is necessary to look first at the changing role of government in education and in particular at moves to allow schools more scope to make their own decisions in curricular matters and in the use of resources.

Central government is involved with education in a number of different ways. It has four basic roles:

a) provider of resources (to schools, pupils or parents);
b) regulator (through blanket regulations applying to all schools or through specific measures focused on particular situations);
c) producer (free of charge through government services, or more or less at cost price through public utilities);
d) contractor (by contracting out to a particular organisation or through the award of licences, "franchising" or leasing).

The regulatory role can be broken down further according to the area of regulation. An initial classification can be based on a simple three-way division: funding, staffing and the curriculum. This type of regulatory activity has generally been highly centralized and detailed. Put negatively, it has left little scope for decisions at the level of the individual school or school board. Throughout the Western world, nevertheless, movements are currently under way which reinterpret and redirect this role. These new interpretations also cover government's role as producer and contractor. As far as funding is concerned there is a movement towards giving schools decentralised budgets. It is possible to distinguish a number of trends which can be expressed in diagrammatic form (see Figure 1).

In the Netherlands there is a move away from the institution-oriented centralised form of organisation towards the institution-oriented decentralised form. At the same time some elements of the consumer-oriented forms are being discussed. This tendency can also be seen in many other Western countries.

In the United States, for example, there are proposals to strengthen the school in its relations with the school board. This will tend to result in the partial replacement of elected district boards by elected boards at individual school level. These school boards will take on school-based rather than district-based budget management, giving them

Figure 1. **Regulation and organisation type**

Area of regulation	Organisation type			
	Institution-oriented		Consumer/Producer-oriented	
	Centralised	Decentralised to school level	Producers as contractors	Consumer-led
Funding	Specified spending	Lump sum to schools	Contracting out to producers	Vouchers to students or parents
Staffing	Centrally administered	School administered	Producers equals staff	Staff hired by consumers or representatives
Curriculum	National (core) curriculum	School-based supplier-determined	Mixed supplier- and consumer-determined	Consumer-determined

increased freedom of expenditure with respect to the budget, and may lead to a form of joint management by headteachers, teachers and parents.

In the United Kingdom school governing bodies are being given considerable responsibility for controlling school budgets. In a number of other European countries there is a similar emphasis on the responsibilities of the individual school.

Given its strong denominational tradition, a strong leaning towards the autonomous school might be expected in the Netherlands as well. In 1988 the then Minister of Education and Science published a memorandum, entitled "Taking schools into the year 2000", to promote just this. It states:

"The autonomous school will be led, under the responsibility of the competent authority, by a professional management team, at home with techniques of management, developments in education, personnel policy and the stewardship of finances, property and equipment. The school management team, together with various members of the teaching and support staff, will develop policies specific to the individual school and directed at achieving educational results of the highest possible quality".

Thus in the Netherlands as well there is a move to decentralise, to deregulate and to strengthen the position of the individual school.

Greater scope for decision-making often comes down initially to the withdrawal of a number of relatively complex sets of regulations. All these sets of regulations, taken together, have resulted in systems which were quite often impossible to implement, and therefore were often simply ignored. By withdrawing regulations the government is seen to be doing less, or doing it in a different way, leaving more to the individual school.

This deregulation affects the three areas which have been identified: funding, staffing and curriculum. We know something about how these three areas are valued by different groups in schools from research into the attitudes of administrators, headteachers and teachers. Generally, so far as regulations on staffing and on the curriculum are concerned, the opinions of management and teachers concur in estimating that they are now at about the right level of detail, although they are difficult to apply.

Regulations relating to accommodation, equipment and funding however are more criticised, especially in vocational education, partly because the funds available are inadequate.

In the Netherlands during the past ten years there has been a debate on the quality of education, which has been conducted over a fairly broad front. The debate is currently raising two questions relevant to regulation:
a) Who determines quality?
b) How can quality be measured?

Further and higher education, and organisations of employees and employers, can be regarded as potential determinants of quality. Encouraging local and regional consultation, drafting job profiles and suchlike are all part of this revitalizing process. Stimulating the generally passive and dutiful parents' associations and turning them into assertive and aggressive consumer organisations also has a role to play. All this can also be expressed in a more abstract way: what we are seeing is the reintroduction of a market mechanism through which parties in the market can determine quality in practice. Thus, who determines quality is no longer a matter of regulation, but a matter of market processes. Moreover, the reintroduction of market forces in the area of educational quality involves new and different ways of determining quality. We have seen in recent years the introduction of new quality control instruments – programme review committees, accreditation procedures, self-assessment, school-based reviews, full inspections, school reports, internal school career studies, pupil monitoring systems, regional comparisons of pupil test results, assessments of one school by another, subject area committees, sector advisory committees – which are all aids to determining quality and until a few years ago were to be encountered only in the scientific literature, and certainly not as subjects of everyday conversation. In short, the debate on quality has not proved barren: a sort of market has grown up and a huge number of quality determination instruments have been developed.

Let us turn now to the funding issues. Until recently the resource allocation system contained a considerable amount of detail. The prescriptive and restrictive effect of all this well-meaning effort was inevitable, and something the educational world could live with. Surprisingly, it was business management experts who came forward with alternatives. To create a systematic approach to funding schools, it is possible to start with the "input side", as has traditionally been done, or with the performance and results of the schools, the "output side".

An analysis of the quality and funding debate in the Netherlands in the past ten years reveals three stages. In the first stage an attempt was made to introduce broader and more general input funding - that is, a move is made from specific grants to broader block grants. This is an important step, and one which has been taken in the present funding system in primary education in the Netherlands. It is also being introduced in secondary education.

In the second stage people try to work out a relationship between funding and the quality of education. Funding is in one way or another geared to performance, the results obtained by schools. Good performance will mean more money and poor performance less money. A better success rate in university education will mean additional resources, for the university in question, as well as fewer early leavers from secondary school.

The question is, how far we can go with this process? Could we also say "better geography exam results, more money"? Who is to define what kinds of performance are to be taken into account in calculating funding, and who is to decide whether – in the face of widely different starting positions of pupils drawn from varying groups within the population – this performance has indeed been achieved by the school, or if the schools are just labelling a difference already present in the population? One solution might be some form of central assessment. But would that not be directly contradictory to the basic principle? Another solution would be to let the market pass judgement: the market of pupils and parents, of further and higher education, and of employers and employees. Funding procedures which combine performance and input in this way have already been attempted. Vouchers are one example of an attempt to achieve funding through the market, and one with which we have some experience in a modified form in this country. With a little imagination, it is possible to think of other forms of funding via the market.

That is the second stage in the relationship between funding and quality. The first was relatively simple. Concentrate on input factors, but make them broader, more general than we used to do. The second stage establishes in one way or another a link between input factors and outcomes or results. And there is a discussion to be had on what is exactly an outcome of a particular school. There is also a third stage in the debate, which is presently under discussion. This third stage involves the direct provision of resources by wealthy parties in the market, without any distribution or redistribution by a government agency. Higher and adult education will probably be the first sector in which this can be put into practice. Donations, sponsorship, loans of equipment, shared use of expensive machines, substantial private contributions, and contract activities, are all examples of this form of funding. It will be clear that the dividing line between public and private education may then be eroded. In this third stage the position of central government is disappearing as it no longer acts as a collecting, allocating or agency.

Thinking about increasing the policy scope for schools in the Netherlands has advanced considerably over the last few years. There has been progress too in creating relevant instruments for quality control and establishing the grounds for funding, but it will take some time yet to achieve fully appropriate instruments for these purposes. At the same time, in the debate about these changes in the relationship between quality and funding, warnings are being sounded against allowing such changes to go too far. To confine quality exclusively to testable results is an extremely unattractive proposition in the long term; it is scarcely a realistic option for primary schools to acquire their own resources; changes in funding methods must not lead to unacceptable differences in funding levels between schools.

Factors that determine quality

What do we know about the determinants of quality? Is there any research which identifies factors in the school which contribute to reaching a certain level of quality? Do these factors have anything to do with the funding system? Can we create a funding system, for personnel costs as well as expenditure on equipment and buildings, that has any influence on any of the factors determining the quality of the educational process? I hope to show that there might be some relationship. If there is not, we are left with a funding system that has nothing to do with the quality of education. From the point of view of an educator, that is hardly an attractive prospect.

Changes which increase the freedom of schools to make their own educational decisions are long-term processes. The resource allocation system currently being used in Dutch primary schools is to some extent keeping pace with these changes. The increase in schools' budgetary freedom is an important link between the increase in policy scope and the funding system.

Research aiming at identifying the differences between "good" and "not so good" schools seemed originally to supply a simple list of criteria on the basis of which schools could be divided into the two categories. This standard list for effective schools usually contains five or six "pointers":

- strong leadership. The headteacher is both the instructional and the administrative leader;
- high expectations of the pupils;
- emphasis on basic skills;
- an orderly environment;
- frequent assessment of pupils;
- emphasis on net learning time for pupils.

Once these six "pointers" had been identified attempts were made to apply them in other schools, hoping that they would bring about an improvement in results. The problem is that various follow-up studies have revealed that these criteria do not always coincide with good school results. For example, the time headteachers spend teaching or providing support for teaching has been shown by several studies to show rather less relation to the effectiveness of the schools concerned than was previously supposed.

In one study of high schools in urban areas characteristics of six areas of leadership were identified and headteachers were asked to indicate the importance of their involvement in them ("leadership rating"). The six areas (improving instruction, consensus on educational objectives, staff development, ensuring financial and other support, involving staff in planning, exercising authority over school policy and organisation) covered both the pedagogical and administrative aspects of school life. The purpose of the research was to discover what action there was in these areas and whether it bore any particular relation to the characteristics of the districts or to pupil results.

It was found that the headteachers varied enormously in the degree of leadership they exhibited in the six areas. Leadership cannot be neatly divided between administrative and instructional or curricular leadership. There were many tasks where the headteachers had little to say or did not score highly because powers resided elsewhere. Most of the headteachers provided active leadership in several respects; 25 per cent of them had a high score on more than half of the indicators. Areas in which headteachers exercised little leadership were those where priorities were set by other local bodies or the national government.

Traditionally, funding of equipment and material is associated with the administrative side of the school. This research revealed that there is a considerable interplay between the administrative leadership in the school and the instructional, curricular side of leadership. A system of funding cannot therefore only be geared to the administrative side of the school. Relationships have to be worked out between ways of funding for equipment and buildings and that for other areas of the school. Although research on effective schools is by no means completed, the provisional outcomes do provide a very interesting set of criteria to assess the possible impact of funding systems on school outcomes.

Funding quality

Although research is still going on it is tempting to draw a number of conclusions about the potential effect of central government action on quality.

At the level of the school community, there are several factors which are not directly amenable to influence by national policy instruments: examples are community spirit, high pupil expectations and parent participation. At the level of the curriculum and the organisation or management of the school, however, there are areas where influence can be exercised. These include:

   a) a degree of autonomy in school management;
   b) coordination of resources to support activities;
   c) in-service teacher training.

The resource allocation system can be established in such a way as to promote these factors. In addition, there are other factors which more directly concern the pupils, such as rules for pupil behaviour, progress reports, school recognition and appreciation of pupil progress, and so on.

Although the present system of funding in the Netherlands was not set up with such objects in mind, it is helping to promote autonomy and a more considered use of resources. How exactly it influences these aspects has so far not been the object of research.

A resource allocation system for education has of course to meet a number of internal requirements: it must, for example, be simple, adequate, and efficient. This paper has not considered those internal requirements but has assessed the funding system on the basis of other criteria. In the first place, a system must be consistent with prevailing policy. At present, in many countries, policy is placing an emphasis on a more distant relationship between government and schools. Giving schools increased scope to make their own policies is the most important way in which this concept is being put into practice.

In the second place, the funding system must, at least indirectly, encourage a relationship with factors that determine quality or effectiveness at the individual school level. We have reviewed a number of different factors that determine quality and noted that some connections exist between the funding system and the quality aspects of education. In the following contributions, these aspects of funding and quality of education will be examined in greater detail and depth.

Resourcing the Curriculum: Furniture and Equipment

J.C. van Bruggen

Is it possible to translate the concept of "good education, meeting the demands of the law" into a well-defined curriculum in terms of aims, objectives, content and classroom organisation? And if such a curriculum exists is it possible to translate it into a well-defined package of teaching equipment and into the money needed to buy such equipment?

To put it more generally: how far is the quality of primary education influenced by the amount of money available for teaching equipment? The preceding chapter discusses the complex and under-researched relationship between management, financing and educational quality. This chapter concludes that it is possible to establish appropriate budgets for teaching equipment, but only in a rough and ready way and in general terms. And that it is better to do so by fixing a baseline budget for reasonable curriculum delivery than by specifying allocations for teaching equipment as such. Other factors, for example in-service training, leadership and school-based curriculum development, are more important.

Defining the curriculum

"Curriculum" is a difficult word, because it is used in different ways in different countries. In the Dutch educational tradition it is most frequently used to denote the collection of ideas about aims, objectives, content, sequence, and principles of delivery of teaching specific to an individual school. For primary schools such a curriculum may be recorded in a document of some 50-200 pages which will include many references to other documents, for example textbooks, teaching manuals, or existing curriculum guidelines. The curriculum and the way in which it is delivered in a school have to meet certain legal specifications, laid down in the Primary Education Act of 1984 and in some additional regulations.

The Primary Education Act however gives only very general rules. As far as curriculum and instruction are concerned, these are of three types:
- *a)* General statements of the aims of education, for example: education must aim at emotional and cognitive development and at developing creativity and the acquisition of necessary knowledge and social, cultural and physical skills.

b) A list of twelve topics and subjects, designated by single words or simple phrases such as "Dutch language"; "promoting social skills, including road safety"; "geography" and so on.
c) Guidance on the interpretation and elaboration of these aims and topics. Considerable freedom is allowed in that process, but the law states that schools must record their interpretations and choices in a school-specific curriculum. This curriculum describes the organization and content of education". The law specifies fairly closely the way in which the curriculum has to be formulated. It can therefore be said that the Primary Education Act lays down no very specific curricular regulations, but does oblige schools to make quite specific decisions.

This curricular freedom can lead to very different interpretations in practice. For example, the law prescribes that some attention must be paid to "science, or at least biology". A school may decide to fulfil this requirement simply by offering some explanatory lessons during the final years of primary education, giving certain information about animals, plants and perhaps stars and electricity. Another school may give more weight to general aims concerning cognitive development and creativity and draw up a very elaborate curriculum for science education, in which laboratory work, field work, experiments, research by children in a school garden, and working with animals are all important elements. It is not obvious that the first school is violating the law or that the second is going further than was intended.

It is therefore possible for a range of different relationships to exist between the legal specifications and the school-specific curriculum. However there are mechanisms which tend to produce convergence in interpretation. These include the initial and in-service training of teachers; past practice, supported by published textbooks; publications on the curriculum from different sources, including the Institute for Curriculum Development; the Inspectorate; tests, published by the Institute for Educational Measurement; and the emerging system of periodic research into the state of the art in different subjects and in different types of school.

There is thus in the Netherlands no defined national curriculum covering the aims, objectives, content and delivery of education. It is therefore difficult to formulate any sort of definition of a specific package of teaching equipment necessary to meet legal requirements. In many other countries such a national curriculum either exists or is emerging. Usually the curriculum defines only objectives and content although sometimes it prescribes a sequence of instruction through grades. In the Netherlands it has been proposed recently that objectives should be prescribed by regulation. That would mark an important move away from traditional curricular freedom. The original proposal developed in 1988 by the Institute for Curriculum Development at the request of the Minister of Education and Science, despite some initial positive reactions, particularly from schools and teachers' unions, has been considerably revised to take account of the fears expressed by local politicians and associations of school boards of an increase in state influence. If the proposals are accepted in their present form there will still be room for local interpretation, and the degree of central steering will remain low.

A common-sense approach

The financial allocation system is based, so far as it concerns teaching equipment, on a two-stage process which goes some way to overcoming the problems discussed above.

In the first stage experienced practitioners are asked to formulate an "educated guess" at a reasonable budget for carrying out a curriculum, on the basis of legal requirements, and current ideas and practice. In the second stage this educated guess is discussed with a second group to see if serious problems either of practice or theory are likely to arise. The initial proposal can then be adapted accordingly. This is a common approach to problems where it is not possible to deduce the correct answer from first principles. It is based on the idea that it is possible to say reasonable things about the legal requirements and about quality in schools and curriculum delivery without founding these statements on solid and generally accepted curricular theory or research.

In practice the system works like this. As we have seen the law refers to "science, or at least biology". This statement may be taken to mean that at least some elements of physics, earth-sciences, geology and chemistry are desirable in the curriculum. Consequently some teaching equipment has to be available: books, instruments, films, material, perhaps some money for excursions. Some equipment for teaching biology is needed. And if biology lessons are to serve the general aims of the law (for example, developing creativity, emotional development) it is reasonable to define the equipment necessary for science education in such a way that some activities such as fieldwork, laboratory work, or working with plants and animals, are possible. Comparing this with the equipment actually used in a sample of schools delivering a curriculum that seems to meet current expectations produces a list of what is needed in the average school. The costs of this equipment can then be fixed as a norm.

There is no reason to think that this approach, based on equity for all schools and on careful consultation procedures, will not lead to an adequate budget for teaching equipment for the majority.

Problems with the common-sense approach

There are problems however. The first arises from the curricular freedom in the Netherlands. It is possible to develop a school curriculum that meets legal requirements and can only be delivered with expensive equipment, for example computers, a school garden, a resource-centre, excursions, a music room, specific materials for reading, arithmetic, geography, history, and so on. A school that develops such a curriculum is acting in accordance with the law, but cannot do what it wants to do because it will not have enough money. Here we see two conflicting consequences of "equality" in the implementation of the law: schools have equal rights to make their own interpretation of the curriculum; and they all have equal budgets. The second equality hampers the realization of the first. Such conflicts are not rare. They arise frequently in relation to rights to housing, work, and health care.

The translation of curricular freedom into decisions about teaching equipment for a particular school suggests a school-by-school approach. This approach has not been chosen, but it could have been. A school's decisions about its curriculum and the equipment necessary to deliver it could be put before a committee. If the committee was satisfied that the school had made a sound curricular choice with a reasonable list of equipment, the committee could decide to fix a budget for the school for a limited period, say four years. During that period the school would be inspected to see whether it had delivered the promised curriculum and made effective use of the budget. This system would respect the principle of curricular freedom better than the current system operating in the Netherlands.

There are objections:
- the choice of equipment necessary for a particular curriculum is in many senses arbitrary and there may be a very human tendency to choose expensively;
- at national level, the budget for teaching equipment would be unpredictable;
- a system of committees and inspectors might be unwieldy and the administrative costs high;
- the system would provide little incentive for cheap, and sometimes elegant, solutions, or for private fund-raising.

A compromise might be to build into the present budget system the possibility for schools which had definite plans about their desired curriculum and the equipment required, to apply to a national or regional committee for extra money to implement it. A spin-off would be the stimulation of new curricular thinking and the development of new equipment.

This approach might also help alleviate a second problem that is inherent in the present budget system, namely the relationship between the budget for teaching equipment and the promotion of the quality of education. The latter is an important goal of educational policy. It is generally accepted that promoting the quality of education has to do with parameters such as:
- the training of teachers;
- the educational environment in the school;
- the instructional methods in use[1].

But can quality of education also be improved by raising the budget for teaching equipment? Or, to look at it from the other direction, how much can government cut the budget for teaching equipment without threatening the quality of education? Everybody will agree that there are some minimum requirements: accommodation, furniture, heating, some textbooks, paper, pencils, some pictures, some maps. But beyond that the arbitrariness of the common-sense approach is so clear that it is difficult to prove that any particular piece of equipment (an overhead projector, a pen instead of a pencil, a museum visit) is absolutely necessary. It is significant that in the relevant literature hardly anything can be found about "teaching equipment" as a factor in school effectiveness.

The same problems of definition that are encountered with concepts such as "a good curriculum" or "a curriculum meeting legal specifications" also attach to the concept of "quality". Quality is certainly broader than "effects in measurable learning results at the end of the primary school period", but even if we restrict our definition to that single, albeit important, indicator of "quality", there is no hard evidence on the question of how far extra teaching equipment improves results. There is no clear and conclusive research matching factors such as teacher quality, curriculum, school leadership, socio-economic background of children with systematically varied elements of teaching equipment. Indeed, such research is hardly possible. The task becomes even more difficult if we consider other indicators of quality.

There are of course many different ideas about the curriculum, all claiming to promote the quality of education. And in some cases these ideas can only be realised with special teaching equipment. Examples are modern language methods which require language laboratories, or discovery learning methods in mathematics and science which require special classroom arrangements and materials.

What we do know is that much depends on the way materials are used: their systematic introduction; the availability of practical advice; their integration into the textbooks and teacher's manuals, are all important. We also know that much of this equipment is used only rarely or not at all once the first flush of enthusiasm is over. The logical conclusion is that general policies for the improvement of quality in education will be better focused on other parameters such as initial and in-service training of teachers; leadership training; and curriculum development.

This does not mean that teaching equipment – beyond the minimum – is irrelevant to the policy objective of improving the quality of education. But defining budgets for teaching equipment as such is an inappropriate instrument for achieving this aim.

Notes

1. Two sources of further reading on this subject are:

    Libermann, A. (1986) (ed.) *Rethinking school improvement* Teachers' College, Columbia University, New York, NY.

    Berg, R. van den, U. Hameyer, K. Stokking (1989) (eds.) *Dissemination reconsidered: the demands of implementation* (ISIP Book 6) ACCO for OECD, Leuven, Belgium.

Resource Allocation for New Construction and Maintenance

G.J. Meijer

In his introductory remarks George Papadopoulos identified the quality of education, effective management of educational resources, and equity and fair distribution of national resources as central themes for this conference.

The resource allocation system for new building and maintenance of primary schools in the Netherlands aims to meet these criteria. The system is based on two assumptions: that money is distributed by central government to be spent locally (for example on new building, or on running existing buildings) in both private and public schools, and that this money is to be distributed in fair proportions.

An analogy can be drawn with the way a parent decides the amount of pocket money for each child. The system is not based on what is actually needed in each individual situation, but on an estimate of typical need. Which expenditures should normally be covered? This depends on what we consider normal. And normal implies norms.

Therefore, a normative funding system has been developed in which the norms are based on models. These models are composed of programmes of requirements in which is set out precisely what is included in the model (in the form of performance specifications or formulae). Ideally this will tell us exactly how much money is needed, and in theory money can be distributed in accordance with the model.

But an ideal world would be a difficult world. Here the difficulty lies in the tension between the degree of detail that is needed (or thought to be needed) to implement the system and the practicality of managing the amount of data that is thus created.

There is a further danger, that the programmes of requirements are taken literally, as cash limits rather than as models. Some managers have thought that it was forbidden to spend more, for example, on energy than the yearly amount that is calculated in the programme of requirements. This underlines the need to make an effort to disseminate information when implementing a new system, in order to inform and where necessary to train the local managers (from municipalities and school boards).

Figure 2 gives an overview of some of the advantages of the global and the detailed approaches to resource allocation.

Whatever the outcome of this discussion, there are some criteria which apply to any resource allocation system. They are:

Figure 2. **Two approaches to resource allocation**

Global approach	Detailed approach
Simpler to manage	Reflects actual needs
Simpler to maintain	Open to discussion by participating organisations
Simpler to keep up-to-date	Central government can specify what money is intended for
Less dependent on data to be collected in the field	Takes account of local experience
Less subject to change (e.g. when new subjects or new teaching methods are introduced)	Sensitive to changing circumstances (new subjects, teaching methods and other)
No pretensions to completeness	Aims at completeness
	Suitable for small schools or municipalities with few schools
	Can be used as a management tool within the school

a) the management (including evaluation and updating) of the system;
b) the relationship between government expenditure and the quality of the school stock;
c) the distinction to be made between existing buildings and new buildings;
d) the relation between models for buildings, new and existing, on the one hand, and the programmes of requirements for maintenance, cleaning and energy on the other.

Management and adjustment of the system

For the successful application of the system, it is essential that the various components (programmes of requirements) remain up-to-date. As the system has been set up in such a way that both quantity and price factors are explicit, it is possible to keep the programmes of requirements up-to-date by adjusting both quantities and prices independently from each other.

As a result, the (annual) government contribution changes, because prices change (owing to wage or price fluctuations) and/or because quantities vary. Quantities may vary when new materials are used, or new building technologies, methods and techniques are applied.

The system may also require modification when the package of activities on which the programme of requirements is based undergoes changes. This may be the case when a new subject or educational programme or even a new teaching method is introduced.

In all these cases, it is possible to indicate precisely where in the different programmes of requirements the necessary changes must be introduced to enable the total allowance to the school to continue to provide realistically for its needs. It is this flexibility and adaptability that constitutes a considerable part of the future value of the system. At the same time however the system becomes rather vulnerable, because of the level of detail required.

Relationship between expenditure and quality of school stock

The system defines the cost centres in terms of quantity and price. It shows how much money is necessary for particular programmes of requirements. As a result it is possible to determine the consequences for the quality of new buildings and the maintenance of older buildings when priorities between the different components of the system change.

The interplay between expenditure and quality is also expressed in the interrelationship between the different programmes of requirements (especially those relating to new building and maintenance). The object of this is to provide an incentive for choosing designs and materials for new buildings such that the total of the capital investment and the subsequent operating costs are brought to the lowest possible level (the life-cycle costing principle). This is a long-term objective. A start has been made in the new system with the explicit description of the different programmes of requirements and maintenance cycles.

The programme of requirements has been defined as a description of the level of material facilities deemed justified by the government. The programme of requirements establishes the standard, that which is necessary to achieve the objectives set, together with the corresponding price.

Existing buildings and new buildings

The distinction drawn between the different kinds of maintenance is based on maintenance cycles: the frequency with which a particular item of maintenance must be carried out.

a) New buildings

For new schools built in accordance with the new resource allocation system the maintenance programme is based on the new-building programme of requirements. This exactly determines the level of facilities for the new building. The government contribution is determined per school on the basis of the standardized quantities.

b) Existing schools

For the existing stock, that is, schools built before the introduction of the new system, the determination of the government contribution must be based on the actual situation. To determine the contribution for existing school buildings the system combines a number of assumptions about the quality of the buildings, and actual measurements (of physical quantities) for each school.

The assumptions are made to limit the number of physical measurements that have to be taken. These assumptions concern:
- *i)* The period at which the school was built. This distinction is important, because different spatial units and different quality standards prevailed at different periods. Differences can be attributed to changes in educational practice (such as the integration between pre-primary and primary education), to developments in architecture and construction technology (such as insulation, the use of low-maintenance materials, or movable walls),and to the introduction of new school concepts (such as the grouping of teaching spaces around a communal area instead of in a row along a corridor).
- *ii)* The surface area of the school grounds (in square metres). This data is necessary to determine the allowances for maintenance, and for property tax.
- *iii)* The surface area of the external wall and the (net) volume of the school building. These data are necessary in order to determine the standardized gas consumption.

The relationship between the models for new and existing buildings and the maintenance programmes of requirements

The determination of the quantities for new buildings and existing buildings is based on models. The models (known as reference models) for existing schools have been developed on the basis of the analysis of a large number of existing schools. The models for the new buildings (known as architectural models) have been made for the calculation of the cost of the establishment. They are not standard designs but graphical models that serve as a basis for calculations.

The contribution for heating costs for new schools is based on the model. A distinction is made between the teaching area and the service areas. Different temperatures are desirable for these two categories of space. The total need for heating can then be calculated. Account is also taken of ventilation, draughts and lighting.

The new building models are also used to determine what the level of insulation should be. This is an important issue, because it is assumed that they meet this standard of insulation when the annual allowance for heating costs is calculated.

Building for Quality: An Architect's View

Th. J. Stroo

We have seen how building is financed under a system in which quantitative regulations are worked out in great detail on the basis of fundamental educational principles. All the quality requirements to which a primary school building must conform are derived from these fundamental principles. In this respect, a distinction can be made between material and spatial quality requirements, although the two frequently overlap.

Material quality, in the sense of the reliable and efficient use of materials, demands not only knowledge of existing materials, but also continuous research and the testing of new possibilities. In this connection, the influence of the chosen designs and materials on maintenance budgets in the short and longer term must not be underestimated.

Material quality is an element of spatial quality. In the Ministry of Education information booklet on the consequences of the building regulations made under the Primary Education Act, those features which help to determine the atmosphere of the school are described as follows:

"**Ambience**: An efficient spatial lay-out can be made on the basis of the fundamental principles, but the ambience of the building must also be taken into account. The school must have a more or less homely atmosphere, in which the child can feel safe and at ease. To guard against creating cold, bare rooms, special attention must be paid, for example, to the choice of building materials, lighting, colour, floors and furnishings, with designated places for the pupils or designated areas in the schools where certain activities always take place."

The spatial quality of a school building is determined by the lay-out of the various spaces, how they are related to each other, by size and scale, light and dark areas, the hardness and softness of colours, and so on. Central to this are the pupils and the teachers who are to use the building.

The younger and older age groups have to be taught in different ways, using methods which address their particular needs. The division of primary education into two stages means that a building must be created that contains two interrelated, but autonomous parts. The location and external appearance of its entrances should not introduce a hierarchy in the ways in which the two groups enter the building. The two external areas should be divided by functional objects, such as a flagpole, or cycle racks, because the younger group will play in the external areas in a different way and at a different time from the older group. Inside the building, the range of requirements can be divided into three types:

i) areas specifically for the lower age group;
ii) areas specifically for the upper age group;
iii) communal areas.

The areas designed for the lower age group will have to be oriented towards smaller scale activities. The identity of an area can be improved by separation. In a vertical plane, too, distinction between high and low can also help to differentiate between various activities.

The areas designed for use by the upper age group should be larger and can also be used for activities involving the whole school, such as weekly assemblies or parties.

If one or more sets of folding doors are located in a communal area, these can be opened to enable the area to be used for parents' evenings or school plays. This creates a certain flexibility, although attention must be paid to technical problems, such as soundproofing.

General areas, such as staff rooms and handicraft areas, will be used by both groups. Depending on the curriculum of the school, these areas can be used to create a more or less clear distinction between the lower and upper age groups.

The character of an area is also influenced by the colours and the materials used. Expressive subjects play a more important role at some schools than at others. The character and identity of a school can be influenced by exhibitions of pupils' work. This possibility must be provided for in the building by, for example, the use of light-coloured brickwork which will bring out the colours in the exhibits and reflect the sunlight. Facing work is suitable for this, since it creates a flat surface and requires a minimum of maintenance.

Accentuated colours in the building – on doors, frames, facades – also serve to increase recognisability. Different colour groups can be used for different areas or to distinguish between age groups.

The exterior of the building (its shape, as well as the colours and the materials used) will determine the identity and image of the school for the community. It is often the case that a school is given a nickname by the community (e.g. "the white school") which proves to be more popular than its official name.

Figure 3 shows the plan of a primary school built according to the principles described above.

Figure 3. **A PRIMARY SCHOOL PLAN**

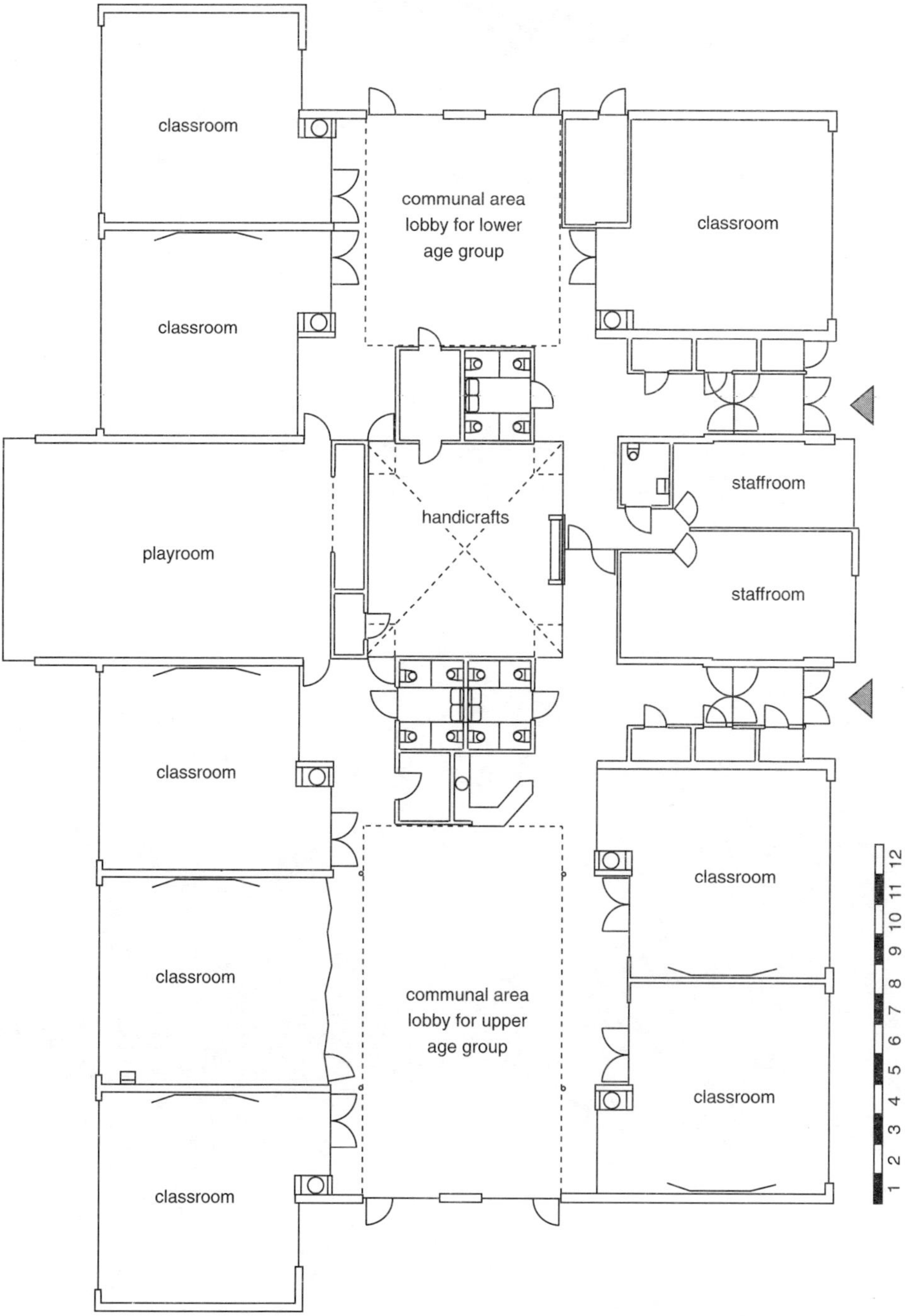

Building for Quality: A Builder's View
H.W.M. Guelen

Three new primary schools

Between December 1987 and August 1989, three primary schools were built in Houten under the new resource allocation system. The schools were commissioned by the Houten Municipal Council and designed by architects Bos & Partners of Baarn. The client and the architects decided to invite a construction company to join them in a building team. After a selection procedure involving a number of companies, Nijssen-Bouw joined the team.

Working on a building team basis means that the builder is involved in the project from the very beginning, and the specific construction techniques employed by the company are taken into account in the design. The construction process is better coordinated from the first to the final stages, with each partner still retaining his own responsibility. Decisions which are made during the preparatory stages can be tested during the execution stage.

During the preparation for building, from programming to delivery, decisions continually have to be made regarding the relationship between the desired quality – either in architectural terms or in terms of the materials and finishes used – and costs. A construction company is able to contribute to the building team specialist expertise, of which familiarity with the costs involved in carrying out a project is an important part. This enables it to give the client and the architect a reliable idea of the relation between the costs and quality of the end product.

The basic requirement for the three primary schools in Houten was that the lay-out of the buildings should be flexible. With their knowledge of the funding system and an analysis of the requirements, the builders were able to assess the design of the three primary schools in the light of the allocated budgets, and to see where the budget might be exceeded. In this way it was possible to give the client and the architect a guaranteed price. If this method is not used during the first stage, the consequences at later stages of the project may be extremely serious.

The cost of the proposed construction methods and materials were weighed up against the quality desired and the resources available. This can be illustrated by a number of examples:

   i) The materials used in the interiors of the buildings were assessed in terms of their maintenance and cleaning costs. With this in mind, for example, sand-lime brickwork was selected for the interior walls.

ii) Plastic sheeting was chosen as outer wall covering. Although this is expensive, it was selected to keep maintenance to a minimum.

iii) In the original design, the span roof construction consisted of truss sections with purlins. In order to reduce costs these were replaced by prefabricated roof sections.

The objective was always to retain the original design of the school. Nijssen-Bouw provided the building team not only with information on costs, but also with advice on the finer details of the design, whereby optimal coordination was achieved between the design and the execution of the project, which in turn affected the quality-cost relationship. This form of cooperation in the building team resulted in optimal coordination between the design and the specific building techniques employed by the company. It also ensured that the budget was not exceeded and eliminated the need to cut costs at the final stage of the preparation process.

The participation of the construction company also enabled the scheduling of the preparation and the execution of the project to be coordinated and guaranteed. The entire preparatory stage lasted for two months.

Advantages for the client

The role of the client in the building process is of the utmost importance, because the partners in the project continually address themselves to the client for important decisions. The client employs three criteria to assess whether the building will actually comply with his wishes – quality, cost and delivery date.

When the partners in a project are working together in a building team, answers to questions regarding these criteria can be given at any time. The building team procedure provides the client with a solid basis for a high quality project with little risk during the execution stage of demands for additional work, or disputes over the interpretation of the specifications, guarantees, or future maintenance. This gives the client greater security concerning the quality of the final product.

Advantages for the designer

In the building team procedure, architects have a more difficult task than usual in some respects and an easier one in others. Price negotiations take place on the basis of analysis, which requires detailed knowledge and expertise in the field of costing. Alternative constructions and/or alterations to the design will more frequently have to be worked out, calculated and assessed.

At the preparatory stage, the procedures for the development of the building plan and the setting of the price are more complex for the architect. During the execution stage, however, the decisions made at the preparatory stage are put into practice. This makes the job easier at this stage, because these decisions have already been made by the team as a whole.

The lesson of the Houten project is that annual maintenance costs are as important as initial building costs. If stricter conditions relating to maintenance were specified in the programme of architectural requirements, this would contribute to a reduction in running costs.

Maintenance Planning

H. Rijken

Prior to the introduction of the new resource allocation system in 1985 planned management and maintenance of school buildings was virtually non-existent, but managers are now increasingly aware that they are essential to keeping school buildings in good condition. The funding system has therefore played a role not only as a key to the distribution of a large amount of maintenance funds, but also as a catalyst in the process of evolution from *ad hoc* to planned maintenance. By no means all building managers have, however, translated this awareness into practice.

In effect, a wide variety of situations exists. Some school boards and local authorities have been working for years on the basis of planned maintenance and have what are sometimes far-reaching cooperative arrangements to ensure the efficient management of school buildings; others plod on with purely *ad hoc* maintenance, without any means of predicting their future situation; and there is every possible variant in between.

Nevertheless planned maintenance has probably evolved further in relation to primary and special school buildings than for any other category of building. The funding system can take some of the credit for this.

In a recent study we noted that, with few exceptions, initial inspection shows maintenance to be clearly in arrears. Even in the first year there are considerable maintenance costs, and if there are no funds available at that time future funds will never be sufficient to eradicate the backlog.

The same study showed that it was possible for school buildings which were originally well designed and subsequently well maintained – both before and after introduction of the funding system in 1985 – to be properly managed and maintained with the resources available through the funding system.

In the many cases where shortcomings have been reported, these have frequently proved to be traceable to the following factors:
- The buildings were originally badly designed as regards their detailing and choice of materials.
- Maintenance has been neglected in the past, so that there is a considerable maintenance backlog which is generally accompanied by expensive consequent damage which must be remedied before "routine" maintenance can begin. In such cases, the funds are frequently inadequate.
- There is inefficient maintenance management, leading to maintenance work being carried out at too high a price or to low standards.

Although the funding system is not intended as such, it is – partly as a consequence of a relative lack of expertise on the part of many building managers – frequently used as the principal guideline in planning maintenance work.

Since the system is strictly normative – geared to a stock of some 11 000 buildings – and since the allocations can be paid out over a fairly lengthy period, building managers would do better to adopt a different approach. To manage buildings properly, managers need plans, and these plans need to be specifically tailored to the building in question. Managers should draw up a multi-year maintenance plan, or have one drawn up for them.

Our method of producing maintenance plans is as follows:

i) Listing the elements likely to require maintenance

Plans of the building provide the necessary quantitative data and at the same time give an insight into the use of materials, detailing, etc.

ii) Inspection of the building

A technical survey gives the necessary qualitative information and insight into the remaining lifetime of the various elements of the building.

iii) Analysis

By analyzing the above data, the need for maintenance, at what intervals, and with what degree of urgency or priority, can be established.

iv) Budget

Data on costs of implementation for a wide range of maintenance operations have been assembled.

v) Draft reports

Besides the maintenance operations mentioned above, the reports contain overviews of the annual costs for each main element (roofing work, painting, etc). In addition, they show income and expenditure and the availability of finance.

This method makes available all the information needed for decision-making. The maintenance plan gives an insight – based on a range of necessary maintenance operations – into the technical maintenance needs of the building and the associated costs; the funding system makes clear what budgets are available now and in the near and more distant future.

Based on this information, decisions can be taken to deploy the resources available in the most sensible way, for example by combining operations, or perhaps delaying them, or by reserving all or part of the funds for use in the future.

vi) Definitive reports

Once the decisions on maintenance expenditure have been taken, the draft report is modified as necessary, and a multi-year plan and a detailed implementation budget for the next plan year are printed out. The implementation budget serves as a guideline for the building manager.

Where a manager is responsible for more than one building, the above steps should lead not only to a plan for each building separately, but also to an overall plan involving the entire building stock. In this situation, there is much greater potential for offsetting financial setbacks caused by poor building or incidental unexpected maintenance expenditure, or for negotiating lower prices for combined operations.

The funding system does in fact assume such large-scale management planning, since the system incorporates a "quantity rebate" of approximately 10 per cent.

The system has proved to be an extremely well thought-out instrument for distributing a large amount of maintenance money among a number of individual school buildings.

The quality of the system is however, in itself, no guarantee of efficient maintenance of buildings, as experience shows. For that, the budget manager also needs appropriate knowledge and experience. It may well take several years before this is recognized. People have to learn the hard way. The funding system is proving to be a major boost to the process of promoting awareness of the need for maintenance planning, for the very reason that is has brought – and is still bringing – building managers face to face with unknown future maintenance expenditure.

Larger organizations will be able to build up such knowledge and experience in-house, or may buy it in. Smaller organizations can combine to form larger management structures in order to achieve economies of scale.

Quality needs to be available at various levels in the organization:
- At policy level there needs to be a clear understanding of the long-term use of individual school buildings. Where any complete or partial change of use is in prospect within the next decade, this will have consequences for maintenance now. The same applies in the case of radical maintenance or renovation. In other words, maintenance of the school building must be seen clearly within a particular context.
- At technical level, sufficient expertise needs to be available to assess the technical merits of the building and to establish when, and with what levels of urgency, particular maintenance operations need to be carried out. This technical data must be translatable into financial data in order to arrive, in consultation with policy makers, at a sensible balance of the operations planned and the financial resources available.
- Again at the technical level, sufficient expertise needs subsequently to be available to ensure correct contracting out of the maintenance work. Important aspects of this are specification of the quality required and acceptable, reasonable pricing. Where this expertise is not available within the management organization, it must be bought in. The funding system makes available resources for this in the form of an allocation for management costs.

Expertise will also be needed in order to enable managers to communicate on an equal footing with the Ministry of Education in the debate on the minimum level of funding necessary for correct and efficient management and maintenance of the schools. The managers and their advisors will be able to make this apparent only on the basis of realistic practical data (preferably over a series of years). To date the funding system can fairly be described as "top-down", but it looks as if the majority of managers of school buildings will have got into the way of planned management and maintenance within the next few years and the "bottom-up" voices will soon be making themselves heard in a more convincing way.

Only when that happens will one be able to say that there is a proper process for evaluating the system in practice. This process must be firmly focused on proper maintenance of school buildings at mutually acceptable costs.

Energy Management
C.C. van Egmond

Energy management is a tool for controlling energy consumption and energy costs. It ensures that energy will be used efficiently and that organisational aims are achieved with minimal cost. The heart of energy management is a systematic approach, which can be presented as a series of steps.

Step 1: Analysis

For all buildings:
- stock-taking of the number of buildings;
- survey of energy consumption and costs;
- comparison of energy costs with available budgets to show over-spending or savings;
- analysis of energy consumption in relation to, for example, the volume or area of the buildings in order to obtain national indicators;
- comparison of typical buildings with national indicators, which gives an idea of the overall potential for savings;
- establishment of priorities for conservation measures;
- detailed analysis of individual buildings.

For individual buildings:
- long range analysis of the different kinds of energy used (consumption as well as costs). By using degree-day method different years can be compared with one another;
- analysis of the energy-saving measures adopted in the past;
- comparison of energy costs with other expenditure, to reveal the relative importance of energy costs;
- analysis of energy contracts and energy bills, over a period of at least one year.

Step 2: Stock-taking (energy balance)

For individual buildings
- Where in the building are the different kinds of energy being used? This is deduced by taking stock of the different energy consumers and by drawing up an energy balance per energy source (gas, oil, electricity, other).

- Which energy consumers have been created and why and how are they adjusted and maintained? The process of stock-taking encompasses all energy consumers, so that the collecting of data regarding adjustment and state of repair can be done simultaneously.

Step 3:   The decision point

Management has to decide whether to set up an energy management system.
- What is the job of the energy coordinator, how much is to be spent on energy management and what returns will it give?

Step 4:   Record-keeping

The need for the recording of consumption data and of data on climate.
- How often and where should records be made?

Step 5:   Evaluation and control of consumption

The framing of standards on which to judge consumption.
- Is consumption too high? If so, why?
- Restraint on consumption follows logically from this.

Step 6:   Reporting

Reporting to management, administrators and occupants of the buildings.

Step 7:   New conservation measures – identification and implementation

- Identification of organisational, technical or behavioural steps to be taken to reduce consumption.
- Identification of necessary investments.
- Framing of an implementation plan.
- Possibility of external support by way of grants or expertise.

Step 1 and step 2 represent the preparatory phase, which is linked by step 3 to the executive phase, steps 4 to 7. From step 7 the system cycles back to step 4.

Energy management remains at all times the responsibility of the managers of a building. Energy management makes it absolutely necessary that one of the members of the management team should take on that responsibility. In a big organisation this task is more likely to be delegated than in a small one, but in every situation the manager will remain the person ultimately responsible.

He should, however, be kept well-informed about the results and the decisions to be taken. If not, the efforts of the energy coordinator will remain largely without effect.

Energy management and the funding system for schools

The funding system is important for energy management in two ways:

a) It establishes annual yearly energy costs and the associated budget.
b) It monitors monthly consumption in relation to the budget.

The following results of energy-audits show how things are working out in practice.

Figure 4. **Budgeted and actual energy consumption**

School	Gas Budget	Gas Actual	Electricity Budget	Electricity Actual	Surplus/shortfall
1	16 560	22 300	2 550	2 500	−6 000
2	11 270	14 500	1 900	1 250	−2 600
3	10 700	9 750	1 600	1 750	+1 800
4	11 950	12 980	2 290	4 120	−2 180
5	11 730	8 400	1 400	1 080	+3 600

By carrying out such energy audits with a cluster of schools, in the same municipality, it can be shown quickly that the situation differs from school to school. Some manage within budget, some do not. In the example shown school 5 managed well within the budget. In this school the parents of one of the pupils took responsibility for energy maintenance. The central heating installation was checked regularly and faults were dealt with competently. The staff were conscientious in their use of lighting. The very fact that someone appeared to be responsible for energy maintenance stimulated the desire to avoid waste.

Using an energy audit, it is possible to make an analysis and to point out how to limit consumption. The following recommendations were offered in order to maximize savings in the schools in the sample.

Figure 5. **Energy-saving measures in five schools**

School	Measure identified	Saving (%)
1	Adjusting optimiser, night-time reduction to 10°C, adjusting switch times	15
	Insulating boilerhouse	3
2	Adjusting optimiser	15
	Minimising ventilation loss	5
	Insulating pipes	3
3	Adjusting optimiser, night-time reduction to 10°C	15
	Insulating valves	3
4	Adjusting optimiser	10
	Insulating valves	3
5	Solving overshoot	3
	Insulating valves	3

Thus in four of the five schools, savings were possible by adjusting controls. Even in school 5, which was well under budget, further savings were possible.

Annex

Issues for Discussion at the Conference

During the conference participants discussed the following questions in five working groups. The conference conclusions are based in part on these discussions.

The general objectives of school planning

The principal legislative acts and regulations and the objectives of education and development policies have both direct, and indirect implications on the the extent of needs and the types of school buildings.

What has been the effect on building needs, and on quality requirements, of recent developments in both quantitative objectives (changes in the number of students to be accommodated, student/teacher ratios) and qualitative objectives (new lines of study, hours, curriculum, pedagogic methods and structure)?

What have been the most important changes in the decision-making process and the distribution of responsibilities in the planning and management of education at the central level, and between the centralised and decentralised levels, and how do they affect educational building?

The assessment of needs and the planning of investments

The objectives of educational policy and decisions about new lines of study and curriculum must be considered in terms of both quantitative and qualitative accommodation needs.

How are existing accommodation capacities and their adaptability assessed? Has decentralisation led to greater or fewer regional disparities? Are there precise measures for compensating for these disparities? How are the needs of the new buildings assessed and how is it decided where to build? When and how are buildings transferred to other types or levels of education? Are maintenance programmes adequate?

When decentralisation has taken place, what powers of decision, financing and consulting have the central authorities kept or developed?

Financing responsibilities and procedures

The transfer of responsibilities is accompanied by changes in the source and procedure of financing.

How has the distribution of costs between national and local authorities evolved in the school building sector? How and in what way are investment resources distributed? How are the costs of projects and subsidies assessed? How are the responsibilities of investment, running and maintenance expenditures distributed? Who has responsibility for the upkeep of buildings?

What is the relationship between those who own and those who use the buildings and how are costs divided between them?

Responsibilities in the school building sector

The changes that have taken place have implications for the distribution of roles among the different authorities and parties involved in school building.

Who drafts pedagogic programmes and construction programmes? How are pedagogical changes taken into account in buildings? How are the architects and builders chosen? Who determines and carries out transformation and maintenance programmes? What are the methods of consulting and who participates?

School building management

There is a widespread trend towards giving more autonomy in the management of school buildings.

How are responsibilities distributed among the governing bodies, those in charge of the school, and personnel? How are budgets established? According to what criteria are loans given and by whom? What are the conditions for opening the building to outside activities and what are the difficulties encountered?

Are specific employees of the establishment assigned to building maintenance? Are they able to seek outside help? If so, where and when?

The implications of recent institutional changes

  i) What effect has the redistribution of policy and financing responsibilities had on regional disparities in terms of equipment, the size and the quality of school buildings, the conditions for use of the buildings, and the conditions applicable to the management of existing stock? Have these changes led to higher costs, and if so, in what areas?
  ii) Is the new distribution of responsibilities considered to be balanced? What are the new methods of cooperation between the different authorities involved? Has

their been a development of specialised groups or consultants on the national or local level?
- *iii)* Is it possible to detect new trends and new problems associated with these changes in responsibilities?
- *iv)* What changes may one expect in the distribution among new constructions, renovations and the development of existing structures? Is there now a better understanding of the costs of using and maintaining buildings? Is there a greater degree of innovation and diversity in building plans than when standard rules or models are applied?
- *v)* Have these changes accelerated, simplified or complicated the process of opening or closing schools, and of responding to needs expressed by users?

Notes on Authors

Thierry MALAN is an Inspecteur général de l'Administration at the French Ministry of Education.

A.M.L. van WIERINGEN is Professor of Educational Administration and Policy at the University of Amsterdam and Managing Director of the Netherlands School for Educational Management.

J.C. van BRUGGEN is Deputy Director for Development at the Dutch National Institute for Curriculum Development (SLO).

G.J. MEIJER is Director of the Information Centre for Schoolbuilding (ICS), Gouda.

Th.J. STROO is Managing Director of the architectural partnership A.A. Bos and Partners B.V.

H.W.M. GUELEN is an employee of the construction company Nijssen Bouw which has been responsible for building over 100 schools in the Netherlands.

H. RIJKEN is head of the property management advisory group of Heidemij Vastgoeddiensten (HVD), Arnhem.

C.C. van EGMOND is a regional network manager for NOVEM (Dutch Energy and Environment Company).

MAIN SALES OUTLETS OF OECD PUBLICATIONS
PRINCIPAUX POINTS DE VENTE DES PUBLICATIONS DE L'OCDE

ARGENTINA – ARGENTINE
Carlos Hirsch S.R.L.
Galería Güemes, Florida 165, 4° Piso
1333 Buenos Aires   Tel. (1) 331.1787 y 331.2391
                    Telefax: (1) 331.1787

AUSTRALIA – AUSTRALIE
D.A. Book (Aust.) Pty. Ltd.
648 Whitehorse Road, P.O.B 163
Mitcham, Victoria 3132   Tel. (03) 873.4411
                         Telefax: (03) 873.5679

AUSTRIA – AUTRICHE
Gerold & Co.
Graben 31
Wien I   Tel. (0222) 533.50.14

BELGIUM – BELGIQUE
Jean De Lannoy
Avenue du Roi 202
B-1060 Bruxelles   Tel. (02) 538.51.69/538.08.41
                   Telefax: (02) 538.08.41

CANADA
Renouf Publishing Company Ltd.
1294 Algoma Road
Ottawa, ON K1B 3W8   Tel. (613) 741.4333
                     Telefax: (613) 741.5439
Stores:
61 Sparks Street
Ottawa, ON K1P 5R1   Tel. (613) 238.8985
211 Yonge Street
Toronto, ON M5B 1M4   Tel. (416) 363.3171
Les Éditions La Liberté Inc.
3020 Chemin Sainte-Foy
Sainte-Foy, PQ G1X 3V6   Tel. (418) 658.3763
                         Telefax: (418) 658.3763

Federal Publications
165 University Avenue
Toronto, ON M5H 3B8   Tel. (416) 581.1552
                      Telefax: (416) 581.1743

CHINA – CHINE
China National Publications Import
Export Corporation (CNPIEC)
P.O. Box 88
Beijing   Tel. 403.5533
          Telefax: 401.5664

DENMARK – DANEMARK
Munksgaard Export and Subscription Service
35, Nørre Søgade, P.O. Box 2148
DK-1016 København K   Tel. (33) 12.85.70
                      Telefax: (33) 12.93.87

FINLAND – FINLANDE
Akateeminen Kirjakauppa
Keskuskatu 1, P.O. Box 128
00100 Helsinki   Tel. (358 0) 12141
                 Telefax: (358 0) 121.4441

FRANCE
OECD/OCDE
Mail Orders/Commandes par correspondance:
2, rue André-Pascal
75775 Paris Cedex 16   Tel. (33-1) 45.24.82.00
Telefax: (33-1) 45.24.85.00   or (33-1) 45.24.81.76
                      Telex: 620 160 OCDE
OECD Bookshop/Librairie de l'OCDE :
33, rue Octave-Feuillet
75016 Paris   Tel. (33-1) 45.24.81.67
              (33-1) 45.24.81.81

Documentation Française
29, quai Voltaire
75007 Paris   Tel. 40.15.70.00

Gibert Jeune (Droit-Économie)
6, place Saint-Michel
75006 Paris   Tel. 43.25.91.19

Librairie du Commerce International
10, avenue d'Iéna
75016 Paris   Tel. 40.73.34.60

Librairie Dunod
Université Paris-Dauphine
Place du Maréchal de Lattre de Tassigny
75016 Paris   Tel. 47.27.18.56

Librairie Lavoisier
11, rue Lavoisier
75008 Paris   Tel. 42.65.39.95

Librairie L.G.D.J. - Montchrestien
20, rue Soufflot
75005 Paris   Tel. 46.33.89.85

Librairie des Sciences Politiques
30, rue Saint-Guillaume
75007 Paris   Tel. 45.48.36.02

P.U.F.
49, boulevard Saint-Michel
75005 Paris   Tel. 43.25.83.40

Librairie de l'Université
12a, rue Nazareth
13100 Aix-en-Provence   Tel. (16) 42.26.18.08

Documentation Française
165, rue Garibaldi
69003 Lyon   Tel. (16) 78.63.32.23

GERMANY – ALLEMAGNE
OECD Publications and Information Centre
Schedestrasse 7
D-W 5300 Bonn 1   Tel. (0228) 21.60.45
                  Telefax: (0228) 26.11.04

GREECE – GRÈCE
Librairie Kauffmann
Mavrokordatou 9
106 78 Athens   Tel. 322.21.60
                Telefax: 363.39.67

HONG-KONG
Swindon Book Co. Ltd.
13–15 Lock Road
Kowloon, Hong Kong   Tel. 366.80.31
                     Telefax: 739.49.75

ICELAND – ISLANDE
Mál Mog Menning
Laugavegi 18, Pósthólf 392
121 Reykjavik   Tel. 162.35.23

INDIA – INDE
Oxford Book and Stationery Co.
Scindia House
New Delhi 110001   Tel.(11) 331.5896/5308
                   Telefax: (11) 332.5993
17 Park Street
Calcutta 700016   Tel. 240832

INDONESIA – INDONÉSIE
Pdii-Lipi
P.O. Box 4298
Jakarta 12042   Tel. 583467
                Telex: 62 875

IRELAND – IRLANDE
TDC Publishers – Library Suppliers
12 North Frederick Street
Dublin 1   Tel. 74.48.35/74.96.77
           Telefax: 74.84.16

ISRAEL
Electronic Publications only
Publications électroniques seulement
Sophist Systems Ltd.
71 Allenby Street
Tel-Aviv 65134   Tel. 3-29.00.21
                 Telefax: 3-29.92.39

ITALY – ITALIE
Libreria Commissionaria Sansoni
Via Duca di Calabria 1/1
50125 Firenze   Tel. (055) 64.54.15
                Telefax: (055) 64.12.57
Via Bartolini 29
20155 Milano   Tel. (02) 36.50.83

Editrice e Libreria Herder
Piazza Montecitorio 120
00186 Roma   Tel. 679.46.28
             Telefax: 678.47.51

Libreria Hoepli
Via Hoepli 5
20121 Milano   Tel. (02) 86.54.46
               Telefax: (02) 805.28.86

Libreria Scientifica
Dott. Lucio de Biasio 'Aeiou'
Via Coronelli, 6
20146 Milano   Tel. (02) 48.95.45.52
               Telefax: (02) 48.95.45.48

JAPAN – JAPON
OECD Publications and Information Centre
Landic Akasaka Building
2-3-4 Akasaka, Minato-ku
Tokyo 107   Tel. (81.3) 3586.2016
            Telefax: (81.3) 3584.7929

KOREA – CORÉE
Kyobo Book Centre Co. Ltd.
P.O. Box 1658, Kwang Hwa Moon
Seoul   Tel. 730.78.91
        Telefax: 735.00.30

MALAYSIA – MALAISIE
Co-operative Bookshop Ltd.
University of Malaya
P.O. Box 1127, Jalan Pantai Baru
59700 Kuala Lumpur
Malaysia   Tel. 756.5000/756.5425
           Telefax: 755.4424

NETHERLANDS – PAYS-BAS
SDU Uitgeverij
Christoffel Plantijnstraat 2
Postbus 20014
2500 EA's-Gravenhage   Tel. (070 3) 78.99.11
Voor bestellingen: Tel. (070 3) 78.98.80
                     Telefax: (070 3) 47.63.51

NEW ZEALAND
NOUVELLE-ZÉLANDE
Legislation Services
P.O. Box 12418
Thorndon, Wellington   Tel. (04) 496.5652
                       Telefax: (04) 496.5698

NORWAY – NORVÈGE
Narvesen Info Center – NIC
Bertrand Narvesens vei 2
P.O. Box 6125 Etterstad
0602 Oslo 6   Tel. (02) 57.33.00
              Telefax: (02) 68.19.01

PAKISTAN
Mirza Book Agency
65 Shahrah Quaid-E-Azam
Lahore 3   Tel. 66.839
           Telex: 44886 UBL PK. Attn: MIRZA BK

PORTUGAL
Livraria Portugal
Rua do Carmo 70-74
Apart. 2681
1117 Lisboa Codex   Tel.: (01) 347.49.82/3/4/5
                    Telefax: (01) 347.02.64

SINGAPORE – SINGAPOUR
Information Publications Pte
Golden Wheel Bldg.
41, Kallang Pudding, #04-03
Singapore 1334　　　　　　　Tel. 741.5166
　　　　　　　　　　　　Telefax: 742.9356

SPAIN – ESPAGNE
Mundi-Prensa Libros S.A.
Castelló 37, Apartado 1223
Madrid 28001　　　　　　Tel. (91) 431.33.99
　　　　　　　　　　Telefax: (91) 575.39.98

Libreria Internacional AEDOS
Consejo de Ciento 391
08009 – Barcelona　　　　Tel. (93) 488.34.92
　　　　　　　　　　Telefax: (93) 487.76.59
Llibreria de la Generalitat
Palau Moja
Rambla dels Estudis, 118
08002 – Barcelona
　　　(Subscripcions) Tel. (93) 318.80.12
　　　(Publicacions) Tel. (93) 302.67.23
　　　　　　　　Telefax: (93) 412.18.54

SRI LANKA
Centre for Policy Research
c/o Colombo Agencies Ltd.
No. 300-304, Galle Road
Colombo 3　　　　Tel. (1) 574240, 573551-2
　　　　　　　Telefax: (1) 575394, 510711

SWEDEN – SUÈDE
Fritzes Fackboksföretaget
Box 16356
Regeringsgatan 12
103 27 Stockholm　　　　　Tel. (08) 23.89.00
　　　　　　　　　　Telefax: (08) 20.50.21

Subscription Agency-Agence d'abonnements
Wennergren-Williams AB
Nordenflychtsvägen 74
Box 30004
104 25 Stockholm　　　　　Tel. (08) 13.67.00
　　　　　　　　　　Telefax: (08) 618.62.32

SWITZERLAND – SUISSE
Maditec S.A. (Books and Periodicals - Livres
et périodiques)
Chemin des Palettes 4
1020 Renens/Lausanne　　　Tel. (021) 635.08.65
　　　　　　　　　　Telefax: (021) 635.07.80

Mail orders only - Commandes
par correspondance seulement
Librairie Payot
C.P. 3212
1002 Lausanne　　　　Telefax: (021) 311.13.92

Librairie Unilivres
6, rue de Candolle
1205 Genève　　　　　　Tel. (022) 320.26.23
　　　　　　　　　　Telefax: (022) 329.73.18

Subscription Agency - Agence d'abonnement
Naville S.A.
38 avenue Vibert
1227 Carouge　　　　Tél.: (022) 308.05.56/57
　　　　　　　　Telefax: (022) 308.05.88

See also – Voir aussi :
OECD Publications and Information Centre
Schedestrasse 7
D-W 5300 Bonn 1 (Germany)
　　　　　　　　　　Tel. (49.228) 21.60.45
　　　　　　　　Telefax: (49.228) 26.11.04

TAIWAN – FORMOSE
Good Faith Worldwide Int'l. Co. Ltd.
9th Floor, No. 118, Sec. 2
Chung Hsiao E. Road
Taipei　　　　Tel. (02) 391.7396/391.7397
　　　　　　　　Telefax: (02) 394.9176

THAILAND – THAÏLANDE
Suksit Siam Co. Ltd.
113, 115 Fuang Nakhon Rd.
Opp. Wat Rajbopith
Bangkok 10200　　　　　Tel. (662) 251.1630
　　　　　　　　　　Telefax: (662) 236.7783

TURKEY – TURQUIE
Kültur Yayinlari Is-Türk Ltd. Sti.
Atatürk Bulvari No. 191/Kat. 13
Kavaklidere/Ankara　Tel. 428.11.40 Ext. 2458
Dolmabahce Cad. No. 29
Besiktas/Istanbul　　　　　Tel. 160.71.88
　　　　　　　　　　　Telex: 43482B

UNITED KINGDOM – ROYAUME-UNI
HMSO
Gen. enquiries　　　　　Tel. (071) 873 0011
Postal orders only:
P.O. Box 276, London SW8 5DT
Personal Callers HMSO Bookshop
49 High Holborn, London WC1V 6HB
　　　　　　　　　Telefax: (071) 873 8200
Branches at: Belfast, Birmingham, Bristol, Edinburgh, Manchester

UNITED STATES – ÉTATS-UNIS
OECD Publications and Information Centre
2001 L Street N.W., Suite 700
Washington, D.C. 20036-4910 Tel. (202) 785.6323
　　　　　　　　　　Telefax: (202) 785.0350

VENEZUELA
Libreria del Este
Avda F. Miranda 52, Aptdo. 60337
Edificio Galipán
Caracas 106　　Tel. 951.1705/951.2307/951.1297
　　　　　　　　Telegram: Libreste Caracas

Orders and inquiries from countries where Distributors have not yet been appointed should be sent to: OECD Publications Service, 2 rue André-Pascal, 75775 Paris Cedex 16, France.

Les commandes provenant de pays où l'OCDE n'a pas encore désigné de distributeur devraient être adressées à : OCDE, Service des Publications, 2, rue André-Pascal, 75775 Paris Cedex 16, France.

Subscription to OECD periodicals may also be placed through main subscription agencies.

Les abonnements aux publications périodiques de l'OCDE peuvent être souscrits auprès des principales agences d'abonnement.

OECD PUBLICATIONS, 2 rue André-Pascal, 75775 PARIS CEDEX 16
PRINTED IN FRANCE
(95 92 01 1) ISBN 92-64-13660-6 - No. 46091 1992